Colli

C000233208

Dec
Tips

Essential advice
on everything from
wallpapering to
sanding and beyond

First published in 2004 by Collins an imprint of HarperCollins*Publishers*
77–85 Fulham Palace Road, London W6 8JB
everything clicks at: www.collins.co.uk

Copyright © HarperCollins*Publishers*
Based on material from *Collins Complete DIY Manual* by Inklink

Project Editor: Claire Musters
Designer: Helen Taylor
Indexer: Kathy Steer

For HarperCollins:

Senior Managing Editor: Angela Newton
Editor: Alastair Laing
Art Direction: Luke Griffin

All rights reserved. No part of this publication may be reproduced,
stored in a retrieval system or transmitted in any form or by any means,
electronic, mechanical, photocopying, recording or otherwise, without
the prior written permission of the copyright owner.

Collins Gem® is a registered trademark of HarperCollins*Publishers*

A CIP catalogue record for this book is available from the British Library

ISBN 0 00 718205 8

Colour reproduction by Digital Imaging
Printed and bound by Amadeus S.p.A., Italy

Please note: Always take care when embarking on any DIY project.
Read the instructions before you commence and take appropriate
safety precautions. Every effort has been taken to ensure that the
information and advice contained in this book is accurate and correct.
However, the publishers can accept no responsibility or liability
for any loss or damage.

If you live outside Britain, your local conditions may mean that
some of this information is not appropriate. If in doubt always
consult a qualified electrician, plumber and/or surveyor.

CONTENTS

INTRODUCTION

Today, DIY is a hugely popular pastime and decorating, in particular, is something most people are keen to do themselves, in order to put their creative stamp on a home.

This book provides all the basic information you need to decorate your home in a small, handy-to-use format. It is organised in helpful colour-coded chapters to enable you to locate the information you need quickly. The book begins by explaining the concepts of colour, texture, pattern and space manipulation and provides decorative scheme ideas for various rooms.

Preparation is one of the most vital parts of decorating, but is often the part of the process that people rush through as they are eager to apply the various finishes they have chosen. The second chapter clearly explains all the preparation that should be done to walls, floors, areas of woodwork, tiles etc., and also details the tools you will need for undertaking decorating jobs. The last two chapters provide extensive advice on applying finishes such as paint, varnish, wall panelling, wallpaper, tiles, wooden flooring and carpets – including tips on how to estimate how much of each material you will need.

PLANNING

The key to a successful decorating scheme is to plan it out well in advance. Makeover magazines and TV programmes can provide some inspirational ideas. You should also carefully consider your use of colour, pattern and space in the room.

SELECTING COLOUR

Developing a sense of the 'right' colour isn't the same as learning to paint a door or hang wallpaper. There are no 'rules' as such, but there are helpful guidelines. In magazine articles on interior design and colour selection, you will find terms such as 'harmony' and 'contrast'; colours are described as tints or shades, and as cool or warm. These terms form a basis for developing a colour scheme.

By considering colours as being like the spokes of a wheel, you will see how they relate to each other – and how such relationships work to create a particular mood.

Primary colours

All colours are derived from three 'pure' colours – red, blue and yellow. These are known as primary colours.

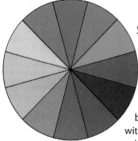

Basic colour wheel

Secondary colours

When you mix two primary colours in equal proportions, a secondary colour is produced. Red plus blue makes violet; blue with yellow makes green and red plus yellow makes orange. When a secondary colour is placed between its constituents on the wheel, it sits opposite its complementary colour – the one primary not used in its make-up. Complementary colours are the most contrasting ones in the spectrum.

Tertiary colours

When a primary is mixed equally with one of its neighbouring secondaries, it produces a tertiary colour.

Warm and cool colours

The colour wheel groups colours with similar characteristics, so on one side are the warm red and yellow combinations. A room decorated with such colours feels cosy or exciting, depending on the intensity of the colours. Cool colours are grouped on the opposite side of the wheel. These blues and greens create a relaxed airy feeling when used together.

USING COLOUR

Pure colours can be used to great effect for both exterior and interior colour schemes, but a more subtle combination of colours is called for in most situations. Subtle colours are made by mixing different percentages of pure colour, or simply by changing the tone of a colour by adding a neutral.

Neutrals

The purest forms of neutral are black and white, from which colour is entirely absent. The range of neutrals can be extended, however, by mixing the two together to produce varying tones of grey.

Neutrals are used extensively by decorators because they do not clash with any other colour, but in their simplest forms they can be either stark or rather bland. Consequently, a touch of colour is normally added to a grey to give it a warm or cool bias, so that it can pick up the character of another colour with which it harmonises. Alternatively, it can provide an almost imperceptible contrast with a range of colours.

Neutrals

Tints

Changing the tone of pure colours by adding white creates pastel colours, otherwise known as tints. Used in combination, tints are safe colours as it is difficult to produce anything but a harmonious scheme, whatever tint colours you use together. The effect can be very different, however, if a pale tint is contrasted with dark tones to produce a dramatic result.

Tints

Shades

The shades of a colour are produced by adding black to it. Shades are rich, dramatic colours, used for bold yet sophisticated schemes. It is within this range of colours that browns appear – the interior designer's stock-in-trade. Brown blends so harmoniously into almost any colour scheme that it is tantamount to

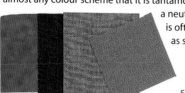

a neutral, and is often used as such.

Shades

USING TEXTURE

We are far more aware of the colour of a surface than its texture, which we almost take for granted – but texture is a vital ingredient of any decorative scheme.

The visual effect of texture is created by the strength and direction of the light that falls on it. A smooth surface reflects more light than one that is rough. Coarse textures absorb light, even creating shadows if the light falls at a shallow angle. Consequently, a colour will look different according to whether it is applied to a smooth surface or a textured one.

Even without applied colour, texture adds interest to a scheme. You can contrast bare brickwork with smooth paintwork, for instance. Like colour, texture can be employed to make an impression on our senses. For example, cork, wood and rugs add warmth to an interior while reflective materials, such as stainless steel and polished stone, give a clean, almost clinical feeling to a room.

USING PATTERN

Fashionable purist approaches to design have made us afraid to use pattern boldly – our less inhibited forebears covered their homes with pattern and applied decoration, with spectacular results.

A well-designed patterned wallpaper, fabric or rug can provide the basis for an entire colour scheme. There is no reason why the same colours should not look equally attractive when applied to the other surfaces of a room, but perhaps the safest way to incorporate a pattern is to use it on one surface only, as a contrast with plain colours used elsewhere.

Combining different patterns can be tricky, but a small, regular pattern often works well with large, bold decoration. Also, different patterns with a similar dominating colour can coordinate well, even if you experiment with contrasting tones. Another approach is to use the same pattern in different colours. When selecting patterns, bear in mind the kind of atmosphere that you want to create.

Patterns add another dimension to a scheme.

MANIPULATING SPACE

There are nearly always areas of a house that feel uncomfortably small or, conversely, so spacious that you can feel isolated in it. Your first reaction may be to consider structural alterations such as knocking down a wall or installing a false ceiling. In some cases, measures of this kind will prove to be the most effective solution – but there is no doubt that they will inevitably be more expensive and disruptive than manipulating space with colour, tone and pattern.

Our eyes perceive colours and tones in such a way that it is possible to create optical illusions that apparently change the dimensions of a room. Warm colours appear to advance – so a room painted brown, red or orange, for example, will give the impression of being smaller than the same room

Warm colours appear to advance.

A cool colour or pale tone will recede.

decorated in cool colours, such as blues and greens, which have a tendency to recede. Tone can be used to modify or reinforce the illusion. Dark tones – even if you are using cool colours – will advance, while pale tones open up a space visually.

The same qualities of colour and tone will change the proportions of a space. Adjusting the height of a ceiling is an obvious example. If you paint a ceiling a darker tone than the walls, it will appear lower. If you treat the floor in a similar way, you can almost make the room seem squeezed between the two. A long, narrow passageway will feel less claustrophobic if you push out the walls by decorating them with pale, cool colours – which will, incidentally, reflect more light as well.

Using linear pattern is yet another way to alter the perception of space. Vertically striped wallpaper or woodstrip panelling on the walls will counteract the

A dark ceiling will appear lower.

A dark floor and ceiling make a room feel smaller.

effect of a low ceiling. Venetian blinds make windows seem wider, and stripped wooden floors seem to be stretched in the direction of the boards. Any large-scale pattern draws attention to itself and – in the same way as warm, dark colours – will advance, while from a distance small patterns appear as an overall texture and so have less of an effect.

Horizontal stripes make a wall seem wider.

Vertical stripes increase the height.

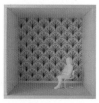

Large-scale patterns advance.

A small, regular pattern recedes.

VERIFYING YOUR SCHEME

Before you spend money on paint, carpet or wallcoverings, collect samples of the materials in order to gauge the overall effect. Start with the more limited choice of furniture fabrics or carpets then collect offcuts or samples of the other materials. Because paint charts are printed, you can never be sure that they will match the actual paint. Usefully, manufacturers often produce sample pots of paint.

Making a sample board

Professional designers create sample boards to check the relative proportions of materials as they will appear in a room. Usually a patch of carpet or wallcovering will be the largest area of colour, while accessories might be represented by small spots of colour. Make your own board by gluing your materials to stiff card in squares or rectangles reflecting their proportions, butting one piece against another to avoid leaving a white border around each sample.

Incorporating existing features

Most schemes will have to incorporate existing features, such as a bathroom suite. Use such items as starting points, building the scheme around them. Cut a hole in your sample board to use as a window for viewing existing materials against those on the card.

SCHEMES FOR LIVING ROOMS

In most homes the living room is the largest area in the house. It is also the room upon which most money is spent in terms of furnishings as well as entertainment units.

Unless you are lucky enough to have more than one reception area, the living room must feel comfortable during the day, relaxing in the evening and lively enough for entertaining. If the room receives little sunlight, a warm colour scheme will help create a cosy atmosphere. Dark, cool tones will produce a similarly snug result under artificial light – but very deep tones can have the opposite effect. Neutral colour schemes are easy and cheap to update in the future by simply changing the accessories.

Curtains and blinds provide the perfect solution to a change of mood. During the day they are not used, but in the evening can become a wall of colour or pattern. Sheer curtains or blinds are also useful. While giving privacy, by screening the view from the window, they also allow daylight to fill the room.

SCHEMES FOR BEDROOMS

A bedroom is first and foremost a personal room so its decor should reflect the character of its occupant(s). It also needs to be relaxing, even romantic. Much depends on the lighting, but pattern and colour can create a luxurious and seductive mood. Few people ever think of using pattern on a ceiling – yet a bedroom presents the ideal opportunity to be adventurous with the decor as you are unlikely to spend much of your waking life there.

Inferior-quality carpeting is often used for bedrooms because it doesn't have to be hardwearing. However, you could give the colour scheme a real lift by investing in an expensive rug or deep-pile carpet.

If a bedroom faces south, early sunlight will provide the necessary stimulus to wake you up, but a north-facing room will benefit from invigorating colours.

Bedrooms sometimes have to serve a dual function. For example, a teenager's room may have to double as a study. Usually a child's bedroom functions as a playroom as well. The obvious choice for decor here would be strong, even primary, colours – but as most children have brightly coloured toys you could use a neutral background scheme.

TIP: The smallest of bedrooms can be made to appear larger by selecting the appropriate colours and tones.

SCHEMES FOR KITCHENS

Kitchens need to be functional areas capable of taking a great deal of wear and tear, so the materials you will use will primarily be dictated by practicalities. However, that does not mean you have to restrict your use of colour. Kitchen sinks and appliances are made in bright colours as well as the standard stainless steel and white enamel, while tiled worktops and splashbacks, vinyl floorcoverings and melamine surfaces offer further opportunities.

Textures are another important consideration. Natural timber remains a popular material for cupboards and will provide a warm element that you can either echo with the paint, paper or floorcovering or contrast with cool colours and textures. Some people prefer to use plastic, ceramic and metallic surfaces for a clean, purposeful look.

TIP: If the kitchen incorporates a dining area, you may decide to decorate the latter slightly differently, so that it is more conducive to relaxation and conversation.

SCHEMES FOR BATHROOMS

Bathrooms, like kitchens, have to fulfil quite definite functions, virtually forcing you to incorporate ceramic, enamelled or tiled surfaces. Imaginative use of tone and colour is therefore especially rewarding, as it can save your bathroom from looking cold or uninviting. A coloured suite and appliances are common but choose carefully, as they are likely to have a dominating influence on all future colour schemes.

Like the bedroom, the bathroom is an area where you can afford to be inventive as it is used only for brief periods. Try to introduce some sound-absorbing materials, such as vinyl or cork flooring, to avoid the hollow acoustics associated with fully tiled bathrooms. Bathrooms are usually small rooms with high ceilings, but painting a ceiling a dark tone, which would improve the proportions of a larger room, can make them feel box-like. A more successful approach here is to divide the walls with a dado rail and use a different colour above and below the line.

TIP: If your home is in a hard-water area, it is best to avoid dark-coloured bathroom suites, as they simply emphasise ugly lime-scale deposits.

PREPARATION

Before you start any decorating it is important to spend time ensuring you have all the right tools and equipment that are required for the job in hand. It is also vital to make sure you leave plenty of time to prepare the surfaces of a room before you apply any paint or other decoration.

DECORATOR'S TOOL KIT

Most home owners collect a fairly large kit of tools for decorating their houses or flats. What follows is a guide to those you will probably find most useful.

Tools for preparation

Whether you're tiling, painting or papering, you need to make sure the surface to which the materials will be applied is sound and clean.

Wallpaper and paint scrapers A scraper is used to remove softened paint or soaked paper. The best scrapers have high-quality steel blades. One with a blade 100 to 125 mm (4 to 5 in) wide is best for stripping wallpaper, while a narrow one, no more than 25 mm (1 in) wide, is better for removing paint from window frames and doorframes. A serrated scraper will score impervious wallcoverings so that water or stripping solution can penetrate faster – but take care not to damage the wall itself.

Vinyl gloves Most people wear house-hold 'rubber' gloves when washing down or preparing paintwork – but tough PVC work gloves are more hardwearing and will protect your skin against harmful chemicals.

Steam wallpaper stripper To remove wallpaper quickly, either buy or hire an electric steam-generating stripper. All steam strippers work on similar principles – a reservoir of water is heated and the resulting steam travels to the steam plate, which is held against the wallpaper to soften it.

Wallpaper scorer A scorer punches minute perforations through the wallpaper so that water or steam can penetrate faster.

Shavehook This is a special scraper for removing old paint and varnish. A straight-sided triangular shavehook is fine for flat surfaces, but one with a combination blade can be used on concave and convex mouldings too.

Straight-sided shavehook

Combination shavehook

Hot-air stripper An electric hot-air stripper is used for softening old paint. With most strippers, you can adjust the temperature and interchangeable nozzles are designed to concentrate the heated air or direct it away from window panes.

Filling knife A filling knife looks like a paint scraper, but has a flexible blade for forcing filler into cracks.

Wire brushes You can use a handbrush with steel-wire 'bristles' to remove flaking paint and particles of rust from metalwork. Alternatively, use a rotary wire cup brush fitted into the chuck of an electric drill. With either method, wear goggles.

Mastic guns Permanently flexible non-setting mastic is used to seal joints between materials with

different rates of expansion, which would
eventually crack and eject a rigid filler.
Mastic can be squeezed direct from a
plastic tube, but using a spring-loaded
gun is easier.

Tack rag A resin-impregnated cloth called a 'tack rag'
is ideal for picking up particles of dust and hard paint
from a surface that's been prepared for painting.

Dusting brush This has long, soft bristles
for clearing dust from mouldings and
crevices before painting.

Abrasives Wet-and-dry abrasive paper
is used for smoothing new paintwork or varnish
before applying the final coat. It consists of silicon-
carbide particles glued to a waterproof backing paper.

Masking tape Low-tack self-adhesive tape is used
to mask off paintwork or glass in order to keep
them free of paint when adjacent surfaces are being
decorated. Wide tape, up to 150 mm (6 in) in width, is
used to protect fitted carpets while skirting boards
are being painted.

Woodworking tools As well as decorating tools,
you will need a basic woodworking tool kit.

Paintbrushes

Some paintbrushes are made from natural animal hair while others are synthetic. All are made of bristle, which is ideal for paintbrushes, since each hair tapers naturally and splits at the tip into even finer filaments that hold paint well. Bristle is also tough and resilient.

Synthetic 'bristle' (usually made of nylon) is designed to resemble the characteristics of real bristle, and a good-quality nylon brush will serve most painters just as well as a bristle one.

Flat paintbrushes You will need several sizes of flat paintbrushes, up to 50 mm (2 in), for painting, varnishing and staining areas of woodwork.

Choosing a brush

The bristles of a good brush – the 'filling' – are densely packed. When you fan them with your fingers they should spring back into shape immediately. Flex the tip of the brush against your hand to see if any bristles work loose. Even a good brush will shed a few bristles at first, but never clumps of bristles. The ferrule (metal band) should be fixed firmly to the handle.

Cutting-in brush The filling of a cutting-in brush is cut at an angle so that you can paint moulded glazing bars right up into the corners and against the glass. Most painters make do with a 12 mm (½ in) flat brush.

Paint shield and scraper There are various plastic and metal shields for protecting glass when you are painting window frames and glazing bars. If the glass does get spattered, it can be cleaned with a blade clipped into a special holder.

Paint shield

Paint scraper

Radiator brush Unless you take a radiator off the wall for decorating, you will need a special brush to paint the back of it and the wall behind. There are two types of radiator brush: one has a standard flat paint-brush head at right angles to a long wire handle; the other is like an ordinary paintbrush but has an angled plastic handle.

Wall brush When applying emulsion paint by brush, use a flat 150 mm (6 in) wall brush.

Cleaning paintbrushes

- **Water-based paints** As soon as you finish working, wash the bristles with warm soapy water, flexing them between your fingers to work the paint out of the roots. Then rinse the brush in clean water and shake out the excess. Smooth the bristles and slip an elastic band round their tips to hold the shape of the filling as it dries.

- **Solvent-based paints** If you're using solvent-based paints (*see* p. 78), you can suspend the brush overnight in enough water to cover the bristles, then blot it with kitchen paper before you resume painting. When you have finished painting, brush out excess paint onto newspaper, then flex the bristles in a bowl of thinners. Some finishes need special thinners – so check for this on the container. Otherwise, use white spirit or chemical brush cleaner. Wash the dirty thinners from the bristles with hot soapy water, then rinse the brush.

- **Hardened paint** If paint has hardened on a brush, soften it by soaking the bristles in brush cleaner. It will then become water-soluble and will wash out easily with hot water. If the old paint is very stubborn, dip the bristles in some paint stripper.

Paint pads

Paint pads help inexperienced decorators apply paints and wood dyes quickly and evenly. Although they aren't universally popular, no one would dispute their usefulness for painting large flat areas.

Standard pads There is a range of rectangular paint pads for decorating walls, ceilings and flat woodwork. These standard pads have short mohair pile on their painting surfaces and are generally made with D-shape handles.

Corner pad A mohair-covered pad wrapped around a triangular applicator spreads paint simultaneously onto both sides of an internal corner. Paint into the corner first, then pick up the wet edges and continue with a standard pad.

Sash pad A sash pad has a small mohair sole and it is used for painting the glazing bars of sash windows. Most sash pads incorporate plastic guides to stop them from straying onto the glass.

CLEANING PAINT PADS

Before dipping a new pad into paint, brush it with a clothes brush to remove any loose filaments.

- When you have finished painting, blot the pad on old newspaper, then wash it in the appropriate solvent – water, white spirit or brush cleaner, or any special thinners recommended by the paint manufacturer. Squeeze the foam and rub the pile with gloved fingertips, then wash the pad in hot soapy water and rinse it.

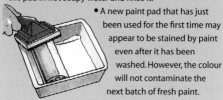

- A new paint pad that has just been used for the first time may appear to be stained by paint even after it has been washed. However, the colour will not contaminate the next batch of fresh paint.

Pad tray Pads and trays are normally sold together as sets. If you buy a separate pad tray, make sure you get one that has a loading roller, as this will distribute paint evenly onto the sole of a pad that is drawn across it.

Extension handles Relatively wide flat pads are made with hollow handles that plug onto extensions to help you to reach up to the ceiling.

Paint rollers

A paint roller is the ideal tool for painting a large area of wall or ceiling quickly. The cylindrical sleeves that apply the paint are interchangeable and slide onto a revolving sprung-wire cage fitted to the cranked handle of the roller.

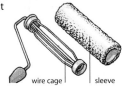

wire cage | sleeve

SIZES OF ROLLER SLEEVES

Sleeves for standard paint rollers are 175 mm (7 in) or 225 mm (9 in) long, but it is also possible to buy 300 mm (1 ft) rollers.

TYPES OF ROLLER SLEEVES

You can buy roller sleeves of various materials to suit different surface textures and kinds of paint. Most sleeves are made of sheepskin or synthetic fibres, cropped to different lengths. A sheepskin sleeve can hold more paint than one that is made from synthetic fibre, but costs about 25% more.

Use a long-pile sleeve for emulsion paint on rough or textured surfaces. A medium-pile sleeve is best for emulsion or satin-finish oil paints on smooth surfaces. For gloss paints, use a short-pile sleeve. A coarse expanded-foam sleeve is good for textured paints.

CLEANING A ROLLER

Remove most of the excess paint from a roller by running it backwards and forwards across some old newspaper. If you are planning to use the roller the next day, apply a few drops of the appropriate thinners to the sleeve and then wrap it in plastic. Otherwise, clean, wash and rinse the sleeve before the paint has time to dry.

- **Water-based paints** If you've been using emulsion or acrylic paint, flush most of it out under running water, then massage a little liquid detergent into the pile of the sleeve before flushing it again.
- **Solvent-based paints** To remove solvent-based paints, pour some thinners into the roller tray and slowly roll the sleeve back and forth in it. Squeeze the roller and agitate the pile with gloved hands. When the paint has dissolved, wash the sleeve in hot soapy water.

Roller tray A paint roller is loaded from a sloping plastic or metal tray, the deep end of which acts as a paint reservoir. Load the roller by rolling paint from the deep end up and down the tray's ribbed slope once or twice, to get an even distribution on the sleeve.

Wallpapering tools

You can improvise some of the tools needed for wallpapering. However, even purpose-made equipment is inexpensive.

Tape measure A retractable steel tape is best for measuring walls and ceilings in order to estimate the amount of wallcovering you will need.

Plumb line Any small weight suspended on fine string can be used to mark the position of one edge of a strip of wallpaper. A purpose-made plumb line has a pointed metal weight called a plumb bob. More expensive versions have a string that retracts into a hollow plumb bob containing coloured chalk, so the string is coated with chalk every time it is withdrawn. When used, it leaves a chalk line on the wall or ceiling.

Paste brush Use either a wide wall brush or a short-pile roller to apply paste to the back of wallcoverings. Clean either tool by washing it in warm water.

Pasting table You can paste wallcoverings on any flat surface, but a purpose-made pasting table provides a convenient working surface. It is only 25 mm (1 in) wider than a standard roll of wallpaper, which makes it easier to spread paste without getting it onto the worktop. The under-frame folds flat and the top is hinged so it is very portable and easily stored in a small space.

Wallpapering brush This is used for smoothing wallcoverings onto a wall or ceiling by squeezing out air bubbles and excess paste. It should be washed in warm water after use.

Seam roller Use a hardwood or plastic seam roller to press down the seams between strips of wallpaper – but don't use one on embossed or delicate wallcoverings.

Smoothing roller Rubber rollers squeeze trapped air from under wallpaper; use felt ones on delicate papers.

Wallpapering scissors These scissors have extra-long blades to achieve a straight cut when trimming wallpaper to the required length.

Craft knife Use a knife to trim paper round light fittings and switches, and to achieve perfect butt joints by cutting through overlapping paper edges. The knife must always be kept extremely sharp to avoid tearing the paper.

Tiling tools

Most of the tools in a tiler's kit are for applying ceramic wall and floor tiles. Different tools are required for laying soft tiles and vinyl sheeting.

Spirit level You will need a spirit level for setting up temporary battens in order to align a field of tiles horizontally and vertically.

Profile gauge This is used for copying the shape of door mouldings or pipework to provide a pattern when fitting soft floor-coverings. As the pins are pressed up to the object, they slide back to replicate its shape.

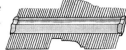

Serrated trowel Make a ridged bed for tiles by drawing the toothed edge of a plastic spreader or steel tiler's trowel through the adhesive.

Tile cutter A tile cutter has either a pointed tungsten-carbide tip or a steel wheel (similar to a glass cutter's) for scoring the glazed surface of a ceramic tile. The tile snaps cleanly along the scored line.

Tile saw A tile saw has a bent-metal frame that holds a thin wire rod under tension. The rod is coated with particles of tungsten-carbide, which are hard enough to cut through ceramic tiles. As the rod is circular in section, it will cut in any direction.

Grout spreader and rubber float The spreader has a hard-rubber blade mounted in a plastic handle. The float looks similar to a wooden float but has a rubber sole. Both tools are used for spreading grout into the gaps between ceramic tiles.

Nibblers It is impossible to snap a very narrow strip off a ceramic tile. Instead, score the line with a tile cutter then break off the waste little by little with tile nibblers. These resemble pincers but have sharper jaws, made of tungsten-carbide.

Tile sander To smooth a cut edge, use either an abrasive-coated mesh or an oiled slipstone.

TILE-CUTTING JIGS

A jig makes it much easier to cut and fit a large amount of tiles (*see* pp 159–60). You can also use a marking-and-cutting jig for the margins around a field of tiles – it will help you to measure the gap and cut the tiles to infill these narrow strips.

- **Using a marking-and-cutting jig** To measure the size of a margin tile, slide the jig open until one pointer is against the adjacent wall and the other is against the edge of the last whole tile. The jig automatically makes an allowance for grouting. Fit the jig over the tile to be cut and use a tile cutter to score the glaze through the slot in the jig.

- **Lever-action jig** If you need to cut a lot of tiles, especially thick floor or wall tiles, buy a sturdy lever-action jig. After pushing the cutting wheel across the tile's glazed surface, simply press down on the lever to snap the tile.

WORKING WITH LADDERS

Whether you need to reach guttering or require a simple step-up to paint the living room ceiling, it is essential to use strong, stable equipment. Working on makeshift structures is inefficient and dangerous. Even for small jobs that don't justify the cost of buying ladders or scaffolding, it's advisable to hire them.

Ladders and scaffolding

Stepladders are essential when decorating indoors. Traditional wooden stepladders are still available, but have largely been superseded by lightweight aluminium-alloy versions. It's worth having at least one that stands about 2 m (6 ft 6 in) high, so you can reach a ceiling without having to stand on the top step. A shorter second ladder may be convenient for other jobs; and you can use both, with scaffold boards, to build a platform. There are many versions of dual-purpose or even multi-purpose ladders that convert from stepladder to straight ladder and can extend considerably. This type of versatile ladder is a good compromise. Sectional scaffold frames can be built up to form towers at any convenient height for decorating inside and outside.

Extending ladder

When you buy or hire a ladder, bear in mind that:

- Wooden ladders should be made from knot-free straight-grained timber.
- Quality wooden ladders have hardwood rungs tenoned through the upright stiles and secured with wedges.
- Wooden rungs with reinforcing metal rods stretched under them are safer than ones without.
- End caps or foot pads are an advantage, to prevent the ladder from slipping on hard ground.
- Adjustability is a big consideration. Choose a ladder that will help you gain access to many parts of your home but will convert to a compact unit for storage.
- The rungs of overlapping sections of an extending ladder should align, or the gap between the rungs might be too small to secure a good foothold.
- Choose an extending ladder with a rope and pulley, plus an automatic latch that locks the extension to its rung.
- Choose a stepladder with a platform at the top to take paint cans and trays.
- Treads should be comfortable to stand on. Ladders with wide, flat treads are the best choice.
- Stepladders with extended stiles give you a handhold at the top of the steps.
- Wooden stepladders often have a rope to stop the two halves sliding apart while most metal ladders have a folding stay that locks in the open position.

How to handle a ladder

Ladders are heavy and unwieldy.
Handle them properly to avoid
damaging property, and to make
sure you don't injure yourself.

Carry a ladder upright, not slung across
your shoulder. Hold the ladder vertically,
bend your knees slightly, then rock the
ladder back against your shoulder. Grip
one rung lower down while you support
the ladder at head height with your other
hand, and then straighten your knees.

To erect a ladder, lay it on the ground
with its feet against the wall. Gradually
raise it to vertical as you walk towards
the wall. Pull the feet out from the wall
so that the ladder is resting at an angle
of about 70°.

How to carry a
ladder safely.

Hold an extending ladder upright while raising
it to the required height. If it is a heavy ladder, get
someone to hold it while you operate the pulley.

Erecting a work platform

Some decorators move a ladder little by little as the
work progresses. However, constantly moving ladders
becomes tedious, and may lead to an accident as you
try to reach just a bit further before having to move

along. It is more convenient to build a work platform that allows you to tackle a large area without moving the structure. You can hire a pair of decorator's trestles and bridge them with a scaffold board, or make a similar structure using 2 stepladders (1). Clamp or tie the board to the rungs and use 2 boards, 1 on top of the other, if 2 people will be using the platform.

An even better arrangement is to use scaffold-tower components to make a mobile platform (2). One with locking castors is ideal.

1 Improvised platform
A simple yet safe platform made from stepladders and a scaffold board.

2 Mobile platform
An efficient structure that is made using scaffold-tower frames.

Decorating in a stairwell

It's not always easy to build a safe platform for decorating in a stairwell. The simplest method is to use a dual-purpose ladder, which can be adjusted to stand evenly on a flight of stairs. Anchor the steps with rope through a couple of large screw eyes fixed to the stair risers; when the stairs are carpeted, the holes will be concealed. Rest a scaffold board between the ladder and the landing to form a bridge. Screw the board to the landing and tie the other end.

Alternatively, construct a tailor-made platform from ladders and boards to suit your staircase. Make sure the boards and ladders are clamped or lashed together securely, and that the ladders cannot slip on the stair treads. If necessary, screw wooden battens to the stairs to prevent the foot of the ladder moving.

Dual-purpose ladder
Use this type of ladder to straddle the stairs, and a scaffold board to create a level platform.

PRIMERS AND SEALERS

Surfaces must be prepared for decoration. This process includes priming and sealing using relevant products.

Stabilising primer Used to bind powdery or flaky materials. A clear or white liquid.
Wood primer Standard solvent-based pink or white primer prevents other coats of paint soaking in.
Acrylic wood primer Fast-drying water-based primer. Some types can be used for undercoating.
Aluminium wood primer Used to seal oily hardwoods and resinous softwoods.
General-purpose primer Seals porous building materials and covers patchy walls and ceilings. Some general-purpose primers are suitable for use on wood, metal and plaster.
Metal primers Essential to prevent corrosion in metals and to provide a key for paint.
PVA bonding agent A general-purpose liquid adhesive for many building materials.
Alkali-resistant primer Used to prevent the alkali content of some materials attacking oil paints.
Aluminium spirit-based sealer Obliterates materials likely to 'bleed' through subsequent coatings, such as metallic paint.
Stain sealer Creates a permanent seal against problem stains such as nicotine, water and pens.

The table below indicates the various surfaces that each of the primers can be effectively used on.

Primers and sealers: suitability, drying time and coverage	Stabilising primer	Wood primer	Acrylic wood primer
SUITABLE FOR			
Brick	●		
Stone	●		
Cement rendering	●		
Concrete	●		
Plaster	●		
Plasterboard	●		
Distemper	●		
Limewash	●		
Bitumen-based paints			
Softwoods/hardwoods		●	●
Oily hardwoods			
Chipboard		●	●
Hardboard		●	●
Plywood		●	●
Absorbent fibre boards	●		
Ferrous metals			
Galvanised metal			
Aluminium			
DRYING TIME: HOURS			
Touch-dry	3	4–6	0.5
Recoatable	16	16	2
COVERAGE (Sq m per litre)			
Smooth surface	6	12	12
Rough/absorbent surface	7	10	10

• Black dot denotes that primer and surface are compatible.

Aluminium wood primer	General-purpose primer	Zinc-phosphate primer	Fast-drying metal primer	Rust-inhibitive primer	PVA bonding agent	Alkali-resistant primer	Aluminium spirit-based sealer	Stain sealer
	•				•	•		
	•				•	•		
	•				•	•		
	•				•	•		
	•				•	•		•
	•				•	•		•
					•		•	
•								
•	•							
•	•							
•	•							
•	•							
							•	
		•		•				
		•	•					
		•	•					
4–6	4–6	4	0.5	2	3	4	0.25	2–3
16	16	16	6	6	16	16	1	6–8
13	12	13	8	8	9	10	4	18
11	9	10	–	6	7	7	3	–

PLASTERWORK

Older houses may have walls clad with slim strips of wood known as laths, which serve as a base for plaster, while newer houses often have plasterboard.

Whatever you intend to use as a decorative finish, a plastered wall or ceiling must be prepared and made good by filling in any cracks and holes.

Tools for filling cracks and holes.

Preparing new plaster

Before you decorate new plaster, if any efflorescence forms on the surface wipe it off with dry sacking.

Once fresh plaster is dry, you can stick ceramic tiles straight on the wall, but always leave it for 6 months before decorating with wallpaper or any paint other than new-plaster emulsion. If you are applying solvent-based paints use an alkali-resistant primer. Size new plaster before hanging wallpaper, or the water will be sucked too quickly from the paste. (Size is a thin gel used for sealing plaster.) If you are hanging a vinyl wallcovering, make sure the size contains fungicide. Mix it with water, following the instructions provided, then brush it on. If you splash it onto painted woodwork, wipe it off with a damp sponge.

Preparing old plaster

Apart from filling minor defects (see p. 46) and dusting down, old dry plaster in good condition needs no further preparation. If the wall is patchy, apply a general-purpose primer. If the surface is friable, apply a stabilising solution. Don't try to decorate damp plaster – cure the cause first.

Preparing plasterboard

Fill all joints between newly fixed plasterboard; then, whether you are painting or papering, daub all nail heads with zinc-phosphate primer.

Before painting with solvent-based paint, prime the surface with one coat of general-purpose primer. When using emulsion, you may need to paint an absorbent board with a coat of thinned paint first.

Prior to hanging wallcoverings, seal plasterboard with a general-purpose primer thinned with white spirit. After 48 hours, apply a coat of size.

Preparing painted plaster

Wash sound paintwork with sugar soap. Use medium-grade wet-and-dry abrasive paper, with water, to key the surface of gloss paint.

If the ceiling is stained by smoke and nicotine, prime it with a proprietary stain sealer. If you want to hang wallcoverings on oil paint, key then size the wall.

Remove flaking paint with a scraper. Feather off the edges with wet-and-dry abrasive paper, then treat the bare plaster with general-purpose primer.

You can apply ceramic tiles over sound paintwork. If there is any loose material, remove it first.

Filling cracks and holes

Special flexible emulsions and textured paints will cover hairline cracks – but larger cracks and holes will eventually reappear if they are not filled adequately.

Rake loose material from a crack with a scraper. Undercut the

Rake out loose material.

edges of larger cracks to provide a key for the filling. Use a paintbrush to dampen the crack, then press cellulose filler in with a filling knife.

Drag the blade across the crack in order to force the filler in, then drag it along the crack to smooth the filler. Leave the filler standing slightly proud of the surface, so that it can then be rubbed down smooth and flush with abrasive paper.

TIP: For deep cracks, build up the filler in stages, letting each application set before adding more.

Patching a lath-and-plaster wall

If the laths are intact, just fill any holes in the plaster with cellulose filler or repair plaster. If some laths are broken, reinforce the repair with a piece of fine expanded-metal mesh. Rake out loose plaster, and undercut the edge of the hole with a bolster chisel.

Staple mesh to stud.

Use tinsnips to cut the mesh a little larger than the shape of the hole. The mesh is flexible, so you can easily bend it in order to tuck the edge behind the sound plaster all round. Flatten the mesh against the laths with light taps from a hammer; if possible, staple the mesh to a wall stud. Patch the hole with one-coat repair plaster. If you want a smoother surface for painting, finish the surface with a thin coat of skimming repair plaster.

Patching small holes in plasterboard

Use plasterer's glass-fibre patching tape if mending holes up to 75 mm (3 in) across. Stick on the self-adhesive strips in a star shape over the hole, then apply cellulose filler and feather the edges.

Alternatively, use an offcut of plasterboard just larger than the hole yet narrow enough to slot through it. Bore a hole in the middle, thread a length of string through and tie a nail to one end of the string. Butter the ends of the

Pull on the string.

offcut with filler, then feed it into the hole. Pull on the string to force it hard up against the plasterboard, then press filler into the hole so that it is not quite flush with the surface. When the filler is hard, cut off the string and apply a thin coat of filler to finish.

Patching larger holes in plasterboard

To patch a large hole use a sharp craft knife and straightedge to cut back the damaged board to the nearest studs or joists at each side of the hole. Cut a new panel of plasterboard to fit snugly within the hole and nail it to the joists or studs, using galvanised plasterboard nails. Brush on repair plaster and smooth it with a plastic spreader or a steel plasterer's trowel.

Cut out the damaged area.

PREPARING WALLCOVERINGS

It's always preferable to strip a previously papered surface before hanging a new wallcovering. However, if the paper is sound you can paint over it. If you opt for stripping off the old covering, the method you use will depend on the material and its condition.

Stripping conventional wallpaper

To soften the old wallpaper paste, soak the paper with warm water and a little detergent, or use a stripping powder or liquid. Apply this with a sponge or houseplant sprayer. Repeat the process then leave the water to penetrate for 15–20 minutes. Use a wide metal-bladed scraper to carefully lift the softened paper, starting at the seams. Resoak any stubborn areas of paper.

Electricity and water are a lethal combination: where possible, dry-strip around switches and sockets. If the paper won't come off, turn the power off at the consumer unit before using any water. Unscrew faceplates to get at the paper behind.

Collect up the stripped paper then wash the wall with warm water containing a little detergent.

Scoring washable wallpaper

Washable wallpaper has an impervious surface film, which you must break through to allow water to penetrate to the adhesive. Use a wire brush or a wallpaper scorer to puncture the surface, then soak it with warm water and stripper.

Peeling vinyl wallcoverings

Vinyl wallcovering consists of a thin layer of vinyl on a paper backing. To remove the vinyl, lift both bottom corners of the top layer of the wallcovering, then pull it away from the wall. Either soak and scrape off the backing paper or, if you want to use it as lining paper, smooth the seams with medium-grade abrasive paper.

Stripping painted wallcoverings

Wallcoverings that have been painted can be difficult to remove. If the paper is sound, prepare it in the same way as painted plaster and decorate over it. To strip it, use a wire brush or scorer to puncture the surface, then soak the paper with warm water and paper stripper. Painted papers (and washables) can easily be stripped, using a steam stripper. Hold the stripper's sole plate against the paper until the steam penetrates, then remove the soaked paper with a wide-bladed scraper.

Using a scorer.

PREPARING WOODWORK

Wooden joinery often needs redecorating before any other part of a house. This is because wood swells when it becomes moist, then shrinks again when it dries out. Paint won't adhere for long under such conditions, nor will any other finish. Wood is also vulnerable to woodworm and rot, so needs careful preparation.

Preparing new joinery for painting

New joinery often comes ready primed, but check it is in good condition. If it is, rub it down with fine-grade abrasive paper, dust it off and apply a second coat of wood primer to areas that will later be inaccessible.

Make sure unprimed timber is dry, then sand the surface in the direction of the grain, using fine-grade sandpaper. Dust the wood down then rub it over with a tack rag or a rag moistened with white spirit.

Paint bare softwood with a solvent-based wood primer or a quick-drying water-thinned acrylic primer. Wash oily hardwoods with white spirit then prime with an aluminium primer. Use standard wood primers for other hardwoods.

When the primer is dry, fill open-grained timber with a fine surface filler. Use a piece of coarse cloth to rub it into the wood, making circular strokes followed by parallel strokes in the direction of the grain. When dry, rub the filler down with a fine abrasive paper.

Fill larger holes, open joints and cracks with flexible interior or exterior wood filler. Once set, sand it flush with fine-grade abrasive paper and dust the surface.

Sealing knots with shellac knotting

Knots and other resinous areas of the wood must be treated to prevent them staining subsequent layers of paint. Pick off any hardened resin, then paint the knots with 2 coats of shellac knotting. If you are going to be using dark colours, you can seal the knots and prime the timber with aluminium wood primer.

Seal resinous knots.

Using grain filler

If you plan to finish an open-grained timber with clear varnish or French polish, apply a grain filler after sanding. Use a natural filler for pale timbers; for darker wood, buy a filler that matches the timber. Rub the filler across the grain with a coarse rag

Applying grain filler.

and leave to harden for several hours, then rub off the excess along the grain with a coarse rag. Alternatively, apply successive coats of the clear finish and rub it down between coats until the pores are filled.

Clear finishes

There is usually no need to apply knotting when you intend to finish the timber with a clear varnish or lacquer. However, for very resinous timbers, apply white (milky) knotting.

Sand the wood in the direction of the grain using progressively finer grades of abrasive paper, then seal it with a slightly thinned coat of the intended finish.

If the wood is in contact with the ground or in proximity to previous outbreaks of dry rot, treat it first with a liberal wash of clear timber preserver. (Check that the liquid is compatible with the finish.)

Cellulose filler would show through a clear finish, so use a stopper to fill imperfections. Stoppers are thick pastes made in a range of colours to suit the type of timber. You can adjust the colour further by mixing in wood dye. As stoppers are oil-based or water-based, make sure you use a similar-based dye.

Sand along the grain.

Preparing man-made boards

Boards such as plywood, MDF, chipboard, blockboard, hardboard and softboard are all made from wood, but they must be prepared differently from natural timber. Their finish varies

Man-made boards

according to the quality of the board: some are compact and smooth, and may even be presealed; others must be filled and sanded.

As a rough guide, no primer is required when using acrylic paints, other than a sealing coat of the paint, slightly thinned with water. However, any nail or screw-heads must be driven below the surface and coated with zinc-phosphate primer to prevent rust stains.

When using solvent-based paint, prime the boards with a general-purpose primer or, for softboard, a stabilising primer. It is best to prime both sides. If presealed, apply undercoat directly to the boards.

Bleaching wood

Unevenly coloured or stained board and timber can be bleached. To avoid a light patch in place of the discoloration, bleach the entire area.

USING TWO-PART BLEACH

To use a proprietary two-part wood bleach, brush one part onto the wood and apply the second part over the first, 5 to 10 minutes later. When the bleach is dry, or as soon as the wood is the required

Bleaching timber.

colour, neutralise the bleach with a weak acetic-acid solution consisting of a teaspoon of white vinegar in a pint of water. Put the wood aside for about 3 days, then sand down the raised grain.

Safety precautions

- Store wood bleach in the dark, out of the reach of children.
- Wear protective gloves, goggles and an apron.
- Wear a face mask when sanding bleached wood.
- Ensure that ventilation is adequate, or work outside.
- Have a supply of water handy, so you can rinse your skin immediately if you splash yourself with bleach.
- If you get bleach in your eyes, rinse them thoroughly with running water and see a doctor.
- Never mix both parts of the bleach except on the wood, and use separate white-fibre or nylon brushes to apply them.

SANDING WOODEN FLOORS

You can turn an unsightly stained and dirty wood floor into an attractive feature by sanding it smooth and clean with hired equipment.

Repairing floorboards prior to sanding

Before sanding, examine your floorboards for signs of woodworm infestation. If necessary, have the boards and the joists below treated with a woodworm fluid.

Replace any boards that have more than a few holes in them – beneath the surface there may well be a honeycomb of woodworm tunnels, and vigorous sanding will reveal them on the surface of the boards.

If you discover dry or wet rot when you lift up a floorboard, get it treated. Look for boards that have been lifted by electricians and plumbers and replace any that are split, too short or badly jointed. Try to find second-hand boards to match the rest of the floor; if you have to use new wood, stain or bleach it to match the floor once sanded.

A raised nail head will rip the paper on the sander's drum, so drive all the nail heads below the surface.

Sink nail heads.

Filling gaps between the floorboards

Many people simply ignore gaps between boards, which is fine, but you will end up with a more attractive floor, as well as improved draughtproofing, if you make the effort to fill the gaps or close them up.

CLOSING UP

Over a large area, the best solution is to lift the boards and re-lay them, filling the final gap with a new board.

FILLING WITH PAPIER MÂCHÉ

If there are only a few gaps, make up a stiff papier-mâché paste with white newsprint and wallpaper paste, plus wood dye to colour match it to the floor. Scrape out dirt from between the boards, and press the paste into the gap with a filling knife. Press it well below the level likely to be reached by the sander and fill flush with the surface, smoothing it with the filling knife.

INSERTING A WOODEN LATH

Large gaps can be filled with a thin wooden lath planed to fit between the boards. Apply PVA adhesive to the gap and tap the lath in place with

Inserting the lath.

a hammer until the wood is flush with the surface. If necessary, skim with a plane. Don't bother to fill several gaps this way: it is easier to close up the boards and fill one larger gap with a new floorboard.

Choosing a sander

The area of a floor is far too large to contemplate sanding with anything but industrial sanding machines. You can obtain the equipment from the usual tool-hire outlets, which will also supply the abrasive papers. You will need 3 grades of paper: coarse, to level the boards initially, followed by medium and fine to achieve a smooth finish.

It is best to hire a large upright drum sander for the main floor area, and a smaller disc sander for tackling the edges. You can sand smaller rooms, such as bathrooms and WCs, using the edging sander only. Hire an upright orbital sander for finishing parquet and other delicate flooring that would be ruined by drum sanding.

Some companies also supply a scraper for cleaning out inaccessible corners. If so, make sure it is fitted with a new blade when you hire it.

Using a drum sander.

Fitting abrasive paper to sanders

Precise instructions for fitting abrasive paper to sanding machines should be supplied with a hired kit. If they are not included, ask the hirer to demonstrate what you need to do. With most drum sanders, the paper is wrapped round the drum then secured in place with a screw-down bar. Edging sanders take a disc of abrasive, usually clamped to the sole plate by a central nut.

Operating a drum sander

At the beginning of a run, stand with the drum sander tilted back so that the drum itself is clear of the floor. Drape the electrical flex over one shoulder to make sure it cannot become caught in the sander. Switch on the machine, then gently lower the drum onto the floor. There is no need to push it as it will move forward under its own power. Hold the machine in check, so that it proceeds at a slow but steady walking pace along a straight line. Don't hold it still for even a brief period, or it will rapidly sand a deep hollow in the floorboards. Take care you don't let go of it, either, as it will run across the room on its own, probably damaging the floorboards in the process.

TIP: Never attempt to change abrasive papers while a machine is plugged into a socket.

When you reach the other side of the room, tilt the machine back, switch off and wait for it to stop before lowering it to the floor (*see also* Sanding the floor).

If the abrasive paper rips, tilt the machine onto its back castors and switch it off. Wait for the drum to stop revolving, disconnect the power then change the paper.

Using an edging sander

Hold the handles on top of the machine and drape the flex over your shoulder. Tilt the sander onto its back castors to lift the disc off the floor. Switch on and lower the machine. As soon as you contact the boards, sweep the machine in any direction, but keep it moving – as soon as it comes to rest, the disc will score deep, scorched swirl marks in the wood. There's no need to press down on the machine. When you have finished, tilt back the machine and switch off, leaving the motor to run down.

Sanding the floor

A great deal of dust is produced by sanding a floor – so before you begin, empty the room of furniture and take down curtains, lampshades and pictures. Sweep the floor to remove grit and other debris. Stuff folded newspaper under the door, and seal around it with masking tape. Open all the windows. Wear old clothes, a dust mask, goggles and ear protectors.

Old floorboards will most likely be 'cupped' (curved across their width), so the first task is to level the floor. With coarse paper fitted to the drum sander, sand diagonally across the room. At the end of the run, tilt the machine, pull it back and make a second run parallel to the first. Allow each pass to overlap the last slightly. When you have covered the floor once, sweep up the sawdust. Now sand the floor again in the same way – but this time across the opposite diagonal of the room. Switch off and sweep the dust up.

Once the floor is flat, change to a medium-grade paper and sand parallel to the boards. Overlap each pass as before. Finally, switch to the fine-grade paper to remove obvious scratches, working parallel to the boards and overlapping each pass. Each time you change the grade of paper on the drum sander, put the same grade on the edging sander and sand the edges.

Even the edging sander cannot clean right up to the skirting or into the corners. Finish these with a scraper, or fit a flexible abrasive disc in a power drill. Vacuum the floor, then wipe it with a cloth dampened with white spirit.

Sand diagonally across the room.

LEVELLING A WOODEN FLOOR

Tiles, sheet vinyl or carpet should not be laid onto an uneven suspended timber floor. Panel over the floor with 3 mm (⅛ in) hardboard or 6 mm (¼ in) plywood.

Conditioning boards

Before you seal the floor with plywood or hardboard, make sure the underfloor ventilation is efficient, in order to prevent problems with damp or dry rot. Also make sure that any underfloor pipework and electric cabling is in good order, as you will not be able to access them easily afterwards.

You must match the moisture content of the board and the humidity of the room, or the board will buckle. If the house is not regularly heated, wet the textured back of hardboard or both sides of plywood with warm water and leave the sheets stacked back-to-back in the room for 24 hours. If central heating is in use just stack the sheets on edge in the room for 48 hours.

Laying the boards

Use chalked string to snap 2 centre lines across the room, crossing at right angles. Cut the boards to form 1200 mm (4 ft) squares. Nail down loose floorboards and sink the nail heads, then plane high points off the surface. Lay the first board on the centre of the string lines, ensuring its edges do not align with the gaps between the floorboards. Unless the manufacturer's instructions state otherwise, lay hardboard rough side up, as a key for the adhesive. Loose-lay the boards: if the margins will be narrow, reposition them.

Nail the first board to the floor with 20 mm (³⁄₄ in) hardboard pins, or use a hired stapler. Start near the centre of the board and fix it every 150 mm (6 in) until you get within 25 mm (1 in) of the edge, then nail around the edge every 100 mm (4 in). Nail other boards butted up to the first (*see* below).

Laying hardboard

1 Snap centre lines.
2 Cut boards into 1200 mm (4 ft) squares.
3 Centre first board.
4 Secure with nails from centre outwards.

5 Butt up other boards, staggering joins. Work round the central board.

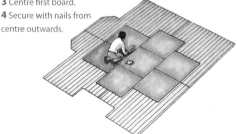

TIP: When levelling a large floor, you can hire a heavy-duty stapler and mallet for fixing the panels to the floorboards.

To cut edge strips to fit the margin, lay the board on the floor touching the skirting but square to the edges of the nailed boards. Hold the board firmly, and use a block of softwood to scribe along it to fit the skirting. Cut the scribed line and butt it up to the skirting, then mark the position of the nailed boards on both sides of the edge strip. Join the marks, then cut along this line. Nail the board to the floor.

1 Scribe to skirting.

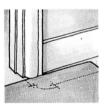

2 Trace frame shape.

To fit into a doorway, butt a board up to the frame and measure to the doorstop. Cut a block of softwood to this size and scribe to the skirting (1). Use the same block to trace the shape of the architrave (2), and cut the shape with a coping

3 Cut and nail down.

saw or jigsaw. Slide the board into the doorway, mark and cut the other edge that butts up against the nailed boards, and then nail the board to the floor (3).

Shortening a door

When you level a floor, you may have to plane the bottom of the door to provide the necessary clearance. Take the door off its hinges and plane towards the centre from each end. Alternatively, ask a carpenter to trim the door *in situ*, using a special circular saw.

Shortening a door.

Laying a base for ceramic tiles

A concrete platform is the most suitable base for ceramic floor tiles, but you can lay them on a suspended wooden floor provided the joists are perfectly rigid, so the floor cannot flex. The space below must be adequately ventilated with air bricks, to prevent rot. Level the floor using 15 mm (⅝ in) marine plywood, screwed down to the joists at 300 mm (1 ft) intervals.

Marine plywood

Floorboards

PREPARING PAINTED AND VARNISHED WOODWORK

Most joinery in homes is painted or varnished and can form a sound base for new paintwork. However, when too many coats of paint have been applied or the paintwork has deteriorated it is best to strip it all off.

Preparing sound paintwork

Wash the paintwork with warm water and sugar soap or detergent. Rinse with fresh water. Rub down gloss paintwork with fine-grade wet-and-dry abrasive paper, dipped in water, to provide a key. Prime any bare patches of wood, building them up gradually with undercoat and rubbing down between each application. Fill open joints or holes with flexible filler. Renew crumbling putty, and seal around window and doorframes with flexible acrylic filler or mastic.

Preparing weathered paintwork or varnish

Unsound paintwork or varnish must be stripped back. There are several methods you can use, but always scrape off loose material first. In some cases, where the paint is very dry and flaky, dry scraping may be all that is required, using a hook scraper and finishing with a light rub down with abrasive paper. Where most of the paint is stuck firmly to the woodwork, remove it using one of the methods described below.

USING A BLOWTORCH

To reduce the risk of fire, before you begin take down curtains and pelmets. You only need to soften the paint with the flame in order to scrape it off. Deposit scrapings in a metal paint kettle or bucket.

Start by stripping mouldings from the bottom upwards. Never direct the flame at one spot, but keep it moving all the time so that you don't scorch the wood. As soon as the paint has softened, use a shavehook to scrape it off. If it is sticky or hard, heat it a little more and try scraping again. Strip flat areas of woodwork using a wide-bladed stripping knife. When you have finished stripping, sand the wood with medium-grade abrasive paper.

You may find it is impossible to sand away heavy scorching without removing too much wood. Sand or scrape off loose blackened wood fibres, then fill any hollows. Prime the scorched areas with an aluminium wood primer then repaint the woodwork.

Using a shavehook.

TIP: Never burn off old (pre-1960s) paint that you suspect may contain lead.

USING CHEMICAL STRIPPERS

An old finish can be removed using a stripper that reacts chemically with paint or varnish. There are general-purpose strippers that will soften both solvent-based and water-based finishes, including emulsions and cellulose paints, as well as strippers formulated to react with a specific type of finish, such as varnish or textured paint. Dedicated strippers achieve the desired result more efficiently than general-purpose ones, but require you to purchase a whole range of specialist products.

Traditionally, strippers have been made from highly potent chemicals that have to be handled with care. Working with this type of stripper means having to wear protective gloves and safety glasses, and possibly a respirator. The newer generation of so-called 'green' strippers do not burn your skin, nor do they exude harmful fumes. However, removing paint with these is a relatively slow process. Whichever type of stripper you decide to use, always follow the manufacturer's health-and-safety recommendations.

Before you opt for a particular stripper, consider the nature of the surface you intend to strip. The thick gel-like paint removers that will cling to vertical surfaces, such as doors and wall panelling, are perfect for all general household joinery. Thinner strippers are perhaps best employed on delicately carved work. For good-quality furniture, especially if it is veneered, make sure you use a stripper that can be washed off with white spirit, as water will raise the grain and may soften old glue.

Working with chemical strippers

- Lay polythene sheets or plenty of newspaper on the floor, then apply a liberal coat of stripper to the paintwork, stippling it well into any mouldings. Leave it for 10 to 15 minutes, then try scraping a patch to see if the paint has softened through to the wood. (Milder strippers will take longer.) Don't waste your time removing the top coat of paint only, but apply more stripper and stipple the partially softened finish back down with a brush, so the stripper soaks through to the wood. Leave it for another 5 to 10 minutes.
- Once the chemical has worked, use a scraper to remove the paint from flat surfaces, and a shavehook to scrape it from mouldings. Wipe it from deep carvings with fine wire wool (when stripping oak, use a nylon-fibre pad impregnated with abrasive material, as it can be stained by steel wool).
- Having removed the bulk of the paint, clean off residual patches with a wad of wire wool, or nylon pad, dipped in fresh stripper. Rub with the grain as you do this.
- Neutralise the stripper by washing the wood with white spirit or water, depending on the manufacturer's recommendations. Let the wood dry out thoroughly, then prepare it the same way as new timber.

USING A HOT-AIR STRIPPER

Electrically heated guns do the work almost as quickly as a blowtorch, but with less risk of scorching. They operate at an extremely high temperature so use them carefully. Some guns come with variable heat settings and a selection of nozzles.

To use a hot-air stripper, hold the gun 50 mm (2 in) from the surface of the paintwork, and move it slowly backwards and forwards until the paint blisters and bubbles. Remove the paint with a scraper or shavehook.

Fit a shaped nozzle onto the gun when stripping glazing bars, in order to deflect the jet of hot air and reduce the risk of cracking the glass.

Old primer can be difficult to remove with a hot-air stripper. This is not a problem if you are repainting: just rub the surface down with abrasive paper. For a clear finish, remove residues of paint from the grain with wire wool dipped in chemical stripper (see p. 69).

Nozzles for hot-air guns

Attachments usually include: a push-on nozzle with an integral scraper (1); a conical nozzle to concentrate the heat on a small area (2); a flared nozzle to spread the heat (3) and a nozzle that protects the glass when you strip glazing bars (4).

PREPARING IRON AND STEEL

Metals are used extensively for window frames, pipework, radiators and door furniture in homes. Metals that are in close proximity to water are often prone to corrosion and require special treatments and coatings.

What is rust?

Rust is a form of corrosion that affects ferrous metals; notably iron and steel. Although most paints slow down the rate at which moisture penetrates, they do not keep it out altogether. A good-quality primer is therefore needed. The type to use depends on the condition of the metal and how you plan to decorate it. Make your preparation of the metal thorough.

Treating bare metal

Remove light deposits of rust by rubbing with wire wool or wet-and-dry abrasive paper dipped in white spirit. For more extensive corrosion use a wire brush or a wire wheel or cup brush in a power drill. Wear goggles while you are wire-brushing. Then use a zinc-phosphate primer on the surface.

Preparing previously painted metal

If the paint is sound, wash it with sugar soap or with a detergent solution, then rinse and dry it. Rub down gloss paint with fine wet-and-dry abrasive paper.

If the paint film is blistered or flaking, remove all loose paint and rust with a wire brush or with a wire wheel or cup brush in a power drill. Apply rust-inhibitive primer to any bare patches, working it well into joints, bolt heads and other fixings. Prime bare metal immediately, as rust can re-form very rapidly.

Stripping painted metal

Delicately moulded sections, for example on fire surrounds, benefit from having old paint and rust that masks fine detail stripped off. Chemical stripping is the safest method for this job – but before you begin, check that what appears to be a metal fire surround is not in fact made from plaster mouldings on a wooden background (the stripping process would play havoc with soft plasterwork). Tap the surround to see if it's metallic, or scrape an inconspicuous section.

Paint the bare metal with a rust-inhibitive primer or a rust-killing jelly or liquid that will remove and neutralise rust. Usually based on phosphoric acid, these combine with the rust to leave it inert, in the form of iron phosphate. Some rust killers deal with minute particles invisible to the naked eye and are self-priming, so there is no need to apply a primer.

Tools for stripping painted metal.

PREPARING OTHER METALS

Non-ferrous metals, such as brass and copper, do not corrode as much as steel or iron, but still need preparing.

Maintaining brass and copper

Ornamental brassware, such as door furniture, should not be painted. Strip painted brass with a chemical stripper. Copper, mainly plumbing pipework and fittings, does not require painting for protection, but visible pipes are often painted to blend in with decor. Before painting, degrease and key the surface with fine wire wool lubricated with white spirit. Wipe away any metal particles with a cloth dampened with white spirit. Apply undercoat and top coats: primer isn't required.

Painting over lead

Before painting old lead pipework, scour the surface with wire wool dipped in white spirit.

The cames (grooved retaining strips) of stained-glass windows and leaded lights can become corroded. Unless the glass is etched or sandblasted, clean the lead with a soap-filled wire-wool pad. Wipe the lead clean, then darken it with a touch of black grate polish on a shoe brush.

Keying lead pipes.

PREPARING TILED SURFACES

Used for cladding walls, floors and ceilings, tiles are made in a variety of materials and in a number of surface textures and finishes. If they become shabby, it's possible to revive their existing finish, decorate them or even stick new tiles on top.

Ceramic wall and floor tiles

Ceramic tiles are stuck to the wall or floor with a special adhesive or, in some cases, with mortar. Removing them in their entirety is messy and time-consuming, but it is often the best solution.

Provided a ceramic-tiled wall is sound, you can paint it with a special-purpose primer and compatible gloss paint. Wash the surface with sugar soap or detergent solution, then apply the primer with a synthetic brush. Leave it to harden for 16 hours, then use a natural-bristle brush to apply the gloss.

You can lay new tiles directly over old ones, but make sure the surface is perfectly flat – check by holding a long spirit level or straightedge across the surface. Tap the tiles to locate any loose ones and either glue them firmly in place or chop

Ceramic
floor tiles

Removing ceramic or quarry tiles

To remove old tiles, first chop out at least one of them with a cold chisel, then prise the others off the surface by driving a bolster chisel behind them. Chop away any remaining tile adhesive or mortar using the bolster. Wear goggles as you remove the tiles, to protect your eyes.

Chopping out the first tile.

them out (*see* box) then fill the space with mortar. Wash the wall to remove grease and dirt.

It is also possible to tile over old quarry or ceramic floor tiles in the same way. Treat an uneven floor with a self-levelling compound. It is not, however, practicable to paper over old ceramic wall tiles.

Polystyrene ceiling tiles

Old polystyrene tiles are usually stuck directly onto the surface with an adhesive that is difficult to remove. In the past, this was applied in five small dabs; a method no longer approved due to the risk of fire. Nowadays, tile manufacturers recommend that a complete bed of non-flammable adhesive be used.

Remove old tiles by prising them off with a wide-bladed scraper, and then prise off the dabs of

Cleaning an old quarry-tile floor

Old quarry tiles are absorbent, so the floor becomes ingrained with dirt and grease. If normal washing with detergent fails to revitalise them, try one of the industrial preparations available to cleaning and maintenance companies. Suppliers of industrial tile-cleaning materials are listed in the telephone directory. Describe the type of and condition of the tiles to the supplier, who will be able to suggest the appropriate cleaner. Loosen stubborn grimy patches by scrubbing with a plastic scouring pad.

Removing dirt.

adhesive. Try to soften stubborn patches of adhesive with warm water or wallpaper stripper, wearing goggles and PVC gloves. One way to give old ceiling tiles a face lift is to paint them. Don't use a solvent-based paint, as it would increase the risk of fire spreading across the tiles. Instead, brush the tiles to remove dust, and then apply emulsion paint.

Vinyl floor tiles

To take up vinyl floor tiles, soften the tiles and their adhesive with a thermostatically controlled hot-air gun on a low setting, and use a scraper to prise them up. Remove traces of old adhesive by applying a solution of half a cup of household ammonia and a drop of liquid detergent stirred into a bucket of cold water. When the floor is clean, rinse it with water.

If vinyl tiles are firmly glued to the floor, you can change the colour with a flexible special-purpose vinyl paint. The floor must be cleaned well, and any silicone-based polish removed with a suitable cleaner. Apply a coat of paint, using a high-density foam roller. Let it dry for 4 hours, then apply another coat. You can walk on the floor in 6 to 8 hours.

Cork wall tiles

Dense prefinished cork wall tiles can be painted directly, provided they are clean and firmly attached to the wall. Prime absorbent cork with a general-purpose primer or, when using emulsion or water-based acrylic paint, thin the first coat to reduce absorption.

Unless the tiles are textured or pierced, they can be papered over – but size the surface with commercial size (see pp 44–5) or heavy-duty wallpaper paste, then apply lining paper to prevent joins showing through.

Mineral-fibre ceiling tiles

Acoustic-fibre tiles can be painted with water-based acrylic or emulsion paint. Wash the tiles with a mild detergent, but don't soak them, as they are absorbent. Conceal stains with an acrylic undercoat.

PAINTING AND VARNISHING

In decorating terms, a finish means a liquid or semi-liquid substance that sets, dries or cures to protect, and sometimes colour, materials such as wood or masonry. Paint is the most commonly used type of finish.

PAINT

Paint is made from solid particles of pigment suspended in a liquid binder or medium. The pigment provides the colour and body of the paint, while the medium allows the material to be brushed, rolled or sprayed; once applied, it forms a solid film.

Common paint finishes and additives

The type of paint you choose depends on the finish you want and the material you are decorating. Various additives modify the qualities of the paint.

SOLVENT-BASED (OIL) PAINTS

The medium for solvent-based (oil) paints is a mixture of oils and resin. A paint made from a natural resin is slow-drying, but modern paints contain a synthetic resin, such as alkyd, that makes for a faster-drying finish. Pigments determine the colour of the paint.

WATER-BASED PAINTS

Emulsion is perhaps the most familiar type of water-based paint. It too is manufactured with a synthetic resin, usually vinyl, which is dispersed in a solution of water. Water-based acrylic paints are primarily intended for finishing interior or exterior woodwork. They tend to dry with a semi-matt sheen.

PAINT ADDITIVES

No paint is made simply from binder and pigment: certain additives are included during manufacture to give the paint qualities such as high gloss, faster drying time and longer pot life, or to make it non-drip.

PAINT THINNERS

If a paint is too thick, it cannot be applied properly. Some finishes require special thinners provided by the manufacturer, but most oil paints can be thinned with white spirit, and emulsions and acrylic paints with water.

GLOSS OR MATT FINISH?

The proportion of pigment to resin affects the way paint sets. A gloss (shiny) paint contains approximately equal amounts of resin and pigment, whereas a higher proportion of pigment produces a matt (non-shiny) paint. By adjusting the proportions, it is possible to make satin or eggshell paints. Matt paints tend to cover best, due to their high pigment content, while the greater proportion of resin in gloss paints is responsible for their strength.

Paint systems

Unless you are using a special one-coat finish, it is necessary to apply successive layers of paint. Painting walls requires a simple system, comprising 2 or 3 coats of the same paint. Painting woodwork and metalwork involves a more complex system, using paints with different qualities (see right).

A paint system for woodwork Different types of paint are required to build a protective system for woodwork.

Bare timber Sand timber smooth; seal resinous knots with knotting.

Primer A primer seals the timber and forms a base for other coats of paint.

Undercoat One or two coats hide the colour of the primer and build a body of paint.

Top coat The final finish provides a wipe-clean coloured surface.

CHOOSING PAINT

Emulsion paint is most people's first choice for internal decorations: it is relatively cheap and practically odourless, and there are several qualities of paint to suit different circumstances. However, some situations demand a combination of paints to provide the required degree of protection or simply to achieve a pleasing contrast of surface textures.

Emulsion paints

Vinyl emulsions are the most popular and practical paints for walls and ceilings. They are available in liquid or thixotropic (thick, non-drip) consistencies, with matt or satin (semi-gloss) finishes. A satin emulsion is less likely to show fingerprints or scuffs. Thixotropic paints are advantageous when painting ceilings.

One-coat emulsion If you are to avoid a patchy, uneven appearance, you need to apply 2 coats of a standard emulsion paint. A one-coat high-opacity emulsion is intended to save you time – but you won't get satisfactory results if you try to spread the paint too far, especially if overpainting strong colours.

New-plaster emulsions These emulsions are formulated for painting newly plastered interior walls and ceilings, to allow moisture vapour to escape.

Anti-mould emulsion
This low-odour emulsion contains a fungicide to ward off mould growth.

Gloss and satin paint

Paints primarily intended for woodwork can also be applied to walls and ceilings that require an extra degree of protection. Similar paints are ideal for decorating the disparate elements of a period-style dado – wooden rail, skirting and embossed wallcovering. Gloss paints tend to accentuate uneven wall surfaces, so most people prefer a satin (eggshell) finish.

Textured paints

Provided the plaster is basically sound, you can obliterate any unsightly cracks with just one coat of textured paint. A coarse high-build paint will cover cracks up to 2 mm (^{1}/₁₆ in) wide. There are also fine-texture paints for areas where people are likely to brush against a wall.

Available in either a matt or satin finish, the paint is normally applied with a coarse-foam roller. Use a synthetic-fibre roller or wall brush if you want to create a finer texture.

The table below reveals what surfaces the various types of paint can be used on. Other information includes the method of application, how many coats are needed and how long each paint takes to dry.

● Black dot denotes compatibility. All surfaces must be clean, sound, dry and free from organic growth.	FINISHES FOR INTERIORS					
	Emulsion	One-coat emulsion	New-plaster emulsion	Solvent-based paint	Acrylic paint	Textured paint
SUITABLE TO COVER						
Plaster	●	●	●	●	●	●
Wallpaper	●	●	●	●	●	●
Brick	●	●	●	●	●	●
Stone	●	●	●	●	●	●
Concrete	●	●	●	●	●	●
Previously painted surface	●	●	●	●	●	●
DRYING TIME: HOURS						
Touch-dry	1–2	3–4	1–2	2–4	1–2	24
Recoatable	4	–	4	16–18	4	–
THINNER: SOLVENTS						
Water	●	●	●		●	●
White spirit				●		
NUMBER OF COATS						
Normal conditions	2	1	–	1–2	1–2	1
COVERAGE: APPROXIMATE						
Sq metres per litre	9–15	8	11	15–16	10–14	2–3
METHOD OF APPLICATION						
Brush	●	●	●	●	●	●
Roller	●	●	●	●	●	●
Spray gun	●	●	●	●	●	

SAFETY WHEN PAINTING

Solvents in paint (Volatile Organic Compounds –
VOCs) contribute to atmospheric pollution and can
exacerbate conditions such as asthma. So where
possible, it's preferable to use paints and varnishes
with low VOC emissions. Most manufacturers label
their products to indicate the level of VOCs.

Safety precautions
- Ensure good ventilation indoors while applying a finish
  and when it is drying. Wear a respirator if you suffer from
  breathing disorders.
- Don't smoke while painting or when near drying paint.
- If you splash paint in your eyes, flush them with water, with
  your lids held open. If symptoms persist, visit a doctor.
- Always wear barrier cream or gloves if you have sensitive
  skin. Use skin cleanser or warm soapy water to remove
  paint from your skin – never use paint thinners.
- Keep all finishes and thinners out of reach of children. If a
  child swallows a substance, don't attempt to induce him
  or her to vomit – seek medical treatment instead.
- Before you wash your brushes and rollers, wipe them on
  newspaper to remove as much paint as possible.
- Ask your local authority about facilities for disposing of
  waste paint and cans.

Preparing paint

Whether you are using paint you've just bought or some left over from a previous job, there are a few basic rules to observe before you apply it.

- Wipe dust from the paint can, then prise off the lid with the side of a knife blade. Don't use a screwdriver: it will buckle the edge, preventing an airtight seal and making subsequent removal difficult.
- Gently stir liquid paints with a wooden stick to blend the pigment and medium. There's no need to stir thixotropic (thick, non-drip) paints unless the medium has separated; if you have to stir it, leave it to gel again before using.
- If a skin has formed on paint, cut round the edge with a knife and lift it out in one piece with a stick.
- Whether the paint is old or new, transfer a small amount into a paint kettle or plastic bucket. Old paint should be filtered at the same time (see below).

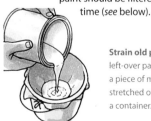

Strain old paint If you are using left-over paint, filter it through a piece of muslin, or old tights, stretched over the rim of a container.

APPLYING PAINT

There are various different methods to apply paint to walls and ceilings, which are detailed below.

Applying paint by brush

Choose a good-quality brush for painting walls and ceilings. (Cheap brushes tend to shed bristles.) A brush about 200 mm (8 in) wide is best, but if you are not used to handling a large brush your wrist will soon tire. You may find a 150 mm (6 in) brush, plus a 50 mm (2 in) brush for the edges and corners, more comfortable, but the job will take longer.

LOADING THE BRUSH

Don't overload a brush with paint; it leads to messy work, and ruins the bristles if the paint is allowed to dry in the roots. Dip no more than the first third

of the brush into the paint, wiping off the excess on the inside of the container to prevent drips. When using thixotropic paint (see p. 85), you should load the brush and apply paint without removing any excess.

Dip only the first third of the bristles in the paint.

USING THE BRUSH

You can hold the brush whichever way feels comfortable to you, but the 'pen' grip is the most versatile, enabling your wrist to move the brush freely in any direction. Hold the brush handle between your thumb and forefinger, with your

Place fingers on ferrule, and the thumb behind.

fingers on the ferrule (metal band) and your thumb supporting it the other side.

Apply the paint in vertical strokes, then spread it at right angles to even out the coverage. Finish oil paints with light upward vertical strokes, to avoid leaving brushmarks in the finished surface. This technique, known as laying off, is not necessary with emulsion.

Applying paint by roller

A paint roller with interchangeable sleeves is an excellent tool for applying paint to large areas. Choose a roller about 225 mm (9 in) long for painting walls and ceilings.

There are a number of different sleeves to suit the type of paint and texture of the surface. Long-haired sheepskin and synthetic-fibre sleeves are excellent on textured surfaces, especially when applying emulsion paint. Choose a shorter pile for smooth surfaces, and when using gloss or satin paints. Disposable plastic-foam rollers can be used to apply some specialist paints, but they soon lose their resilience and have a tendency to skid across the wall.

USING A ROLLER

You will need a special paint tray to load a roller. Dip the sleeve lightly into the paint reservoir, then roll it gently onto the ribbed part of the tray to coat the roller evenly (1). Use zigzag strokes with a roller (2), painting the surface in all directions to achieve even coverage. Keep the roller on the surface at all times – if you let it spin at the end of a stroke, it will spatter paint. When applying solvent-based paint, finish in one direction, preferably towards prevailing light.

1 Dip the roller in the paint, then roll it on the ribbed tray.

2 Apply the paint to the surface in zigzags for even coverage.

Special rollers
Rollers with long detachable extension handles are ideal for painting ceilings without having to erect work platforms. Narrow rollers for painting behind radiators are invaluable if the radiators cannot be removed.

Applying paint by pad

Paint pads for large surfaces have flat rectangular faces covered with a short mohair pile. A pad about 200 mm (8 in) long is best for applying paint to walls and ceilings. You will also need a small pad or paintbrush for cutting in (*see* p. 90) at corners and ceilings.

USING A PAINT PAD
Load a paint pad from its own tray, drawing the pad across the roller so that you pick up an even amount of paint. To apply the paint consistently, keep the pad flat on the wall and sweep it gently and evenly in all directions. To prevent streaking, finish with vertical strokes when using solvent-based paints.

Loading a paint pad.

TIP: As even the best professionals will drip paint at some point, always start with the ceiling before the walls. Make sure you have covered the floor with dustsheets before you begin painting.

Painting the ceiling

Start by erecting a work platform, placing it so that you can cover as much of the surface as possible without changing position. Ceilings can be painted with an extendable roller but you will still need to begin by 'cutting in' as no roller will go right into the edges. This process involves carefully painting along the edges of the ceiling using a small paintbrush.

Working from the wet edges, paint in bands 600 mm (2 ft) wide, working away from the light. Whether you are using a brush, pad or roller, apply each fresh load of paint just clear of the previous application, then blend in the junctions for even coverage.

Paint around the edges.

Blend in the wet edges.

Painting the walls

Use a small brush to paint the edges. If you are right-handed, work from right to left; and vice versa. Paint 600 mm (2 ft) square at a time. Paint emulsion in horizontal bands (1) but gloss in vertical strips (2), because the junctions are likely to show unless you blend in the edges quickly. Finish a whole wall before you take a break, otherwise a change of tone may show.

1 Paint emulsion in horizontal bands.

2 Apply gloss paints in vertical strips.

Painting around electrical fittings

Switch off the electricity at the mains. Then unscrew a ceiling-rose cover so that you can paint right up to the backplate with a small brush. Loosen the faceplate or mounting box of socket outlets and switches so that you can paint behind them.

Using textured paints

Textured paints can be obtained as a dry powder for mixing with warm water or in a ready-mixed form for direct application from the tub. They are available in a range of standard colours, but if none of them suits your decorative scheme you can use ordinary emulsion as a finish over the top.

Using rollers, scrapers or improvised tools, you can produce a variety of textures (see right). It's advisable to restrict distinctly raised textures with sharp edges to areas where you are unlikely to rub against the wall.

APPLYING THE PAINT

You can apply the textured paint using a roller or broad wall brush, but finer textures are possible with the brush. (Buy a special roller if recommended by the paint manufacturer.) With a well-loaded roller, apply a generous coat in a band 600 mm (2 ft) wide across the ceiling or down a wall. Don't press too hard, and vary the angle of the stroke. If you decide to brush the paint on, don't spread it out like normal paint. Instead, lay it on with one stroke and spread it back again with 1 or 2 strokes only.

Texture the first band, then apply a second band and blend them together before texturing the latter. Continue in this way until the surface is covered. Keep the room ventilated until the paint has hardened.

Painting around fittings Mask off the edges of electrical fittings then use a small paintbrush to fill in around and along the edges, trying to copy the texture that has been used on the surrounding wall or ceiling. Some people prefer to form a distinct margin around fittings by drawing a small paintbrush along the perimeter to give a perfectly smooth finish.

Use a small paintbrush to create a smooth finish.

Creating a texture You can experiment with a variety of tools to make any number of different textures. For example, you could try either a coarse expanded-foam roller or one that has a special surface to produce diagonal or diamond patterns. Alternatively, you can apply a swirling, ripple or stipple finish to your walls by using improvised equipment such as a scrunched up plastic bag, an old rag or even a damp sponge.

Creating patterns using a foam roller.

FINISHING WOODWORK

Paint is the most common finish for woodwork, as it offers a protective coating in a choice of colours and surface finishes. However, stains, varnishes, lacquers and polishes give an attractive, durable finish to joinery, enhancing the colour of the woodwork without obliterating the beauty of its grain. When choosing a finish, bear in mind the location of the woodwork and the amount of wear it is likely to get. For example, a finish used in a bathroom will need to be able to endure wet conditions.

The text below introduces a comprehensive range of finishes for protecting and decorating woodwork. Each has qualities that render it suitable for a particular purpose, although many of them can be employed simply for their attractive appearance.

Solvent-based paints

Traditional solvent-based (oil) paints are available in high-gloss and satin finishes, with both liquid and thixotropic (see p. 85) consistencies. They will last for years, with only the occasional wash-down to remove fingermarks needed, but 1 or 2 undercoats are essential. Newer one-coat paints, which have a creamy consistency and high-pigment content, can protect primed wood or obliterate existing colours without undercoating. Apply paint liberally and allow it to flow freely rather than brushing it out like a conventional oil paint. Low-odour solvent-based finishes have largely eradicated the smell and fumes associated with drying paint.

Acrylic paints

These have several advantages over conventional oil paint. Being water-based, they are non-flammable, practically odourless and constitute less of a risk to health and to the environment. They also dry quickly. However, this means you have to work swiftly, to avoid leaving brushmarks.

Provided they are applied to prepared wood or keyed paintwork, acrylic paints form a tough yet flexible coating that resists cracking and peeling. However, acrylic paints will not dry satisfactorily if they are applied on a damp or humid day. Even under perfect conditions, don't expect to achieve a high-gloss finish.

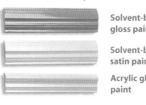

Solvent-based gloss paint

Solvent-based satin paint

Acrylic gloss paint

Wood dyes

Unlike paint, which after the initial priming coat rests on the surface of timber, a dye penetrates the wood. Its main advantage is to enhance the natural colour of the woodwork or to unify the slight variation in colour found in even the same species.

Water-based and oil-based dyes are available ready for use. You can also buy powdered pigments for mixing with methylated spirit. You will have to seal all types with a clear varnish or polish.

Unsealed wood dye

Protective wood stains

The natural colour of wood can be enhanced with protective wood stains. Being moisture-vapour permeable, they allow the wood to breathe while providing a satin finish that resists flaking and peeling.

Protective wood stains are brushed onto the wood. Some manufacturers recommend 2 to 3 coats, while others offer a one-coat finish. Some ranges include a clear finish for redecorating previously stained woodwork without darkening the existing colour. Water-based stains dry faster than those thinned with a spirit solvent.

Protective wood stain

Wood preservers

Wall cladding is often left unpainted, and yet it still needs protection. For this, use a wood preserver, which penetrates deeply into the timber to prevent rot and insect attack. There are clear preservers, plus a range of natural-wood colours.

Traditional preservers have a strong, unpleasant smell and are harmful to plants, whereas most modern low-odour solvent-based and water-based preservers are perfectly safe.

Coloured preserver

Varnishes

Varnish is a clear protective coating for timber. Most modern varnishes are made with polyurethane resins to provide a waterproof, scratchproof and heat-resistant finish. They come in high-gloss, satin or matt. Some are designed to provide a clear finish with a hint of colour. Unlike a wood dye, a coloured varnish does not sink into the timber – so there may be loss of colour in areas of heavy wear or abrasion unless you apply extra coats of clear varnish. Fast-drying acrylic varnishes are opaque when applied, but transparent when dry.

Satin polyurethane varnish

Cold-cure lacquer

This plastic coating is mixed with a hardener just before it is used. It is extremely durable (even on floors) and is resistant to heat and alcohol. The standard type dries to a high gloss, which can be burnished to a lacquer-like finish if required. There is also a matt-finish grade, though a smoother matt surface can be obtained by rubbing down the gloss coating with fine steel wool dipped in wax. Black, white and clear varieties of cold-cure lacquer are available.

Cold-cure lacquer

Finishing oil

Oil is a subtle finish that soaks into the wood, leaving a mellow sheen on the surface. Traditional linseed oil remains sticky for hours, whereas a modern oil will dry in about an hour and provides a tougher, more durable finish. Finishing oil can be used on softwood as well as open-grained oily hardwoods such as teak or afrormosia.

Thick gelled oil is applied like a wax polish (*see* right), and can be used on bare wood or over varnish and lacquer.

Oil finish

Wax polishes

Wax can be employed to preserve and maintain another finish or as a finish itself. A good wax should be a blend of beeswax and a hard polishing wax such as carnauba. Some contain silicones to make it easier to achieve a high gloss. Wax polish may be white or tinted various shades of brown to darken the wood. Although very attractive, it is not particularly durable.

Wax polish

French polish

French polish is a specialised wood finish made by dissolving shellac in alcohol. It is easily scratched, and alcohol or water will etch the surface, leaving white stains. This means it can be used only on furniture unlikely to receive normal wear and tear. There are several varieties. Reddish-brown button polish is the best-quality standard polish. It is bleached to make white polish for light-coloured woods, and if the natural wax is removed a transparent polish is produced. For mahogany, choose a dark-red garnet polish.

Button polish

Garnet polish

White polish

The table below indicates the various surfaces that each of the woodwork finishes can be effectively used on. As well as detailing how the finishes should be applied the chart includes other useful information

● Black dot denotes compatibility. All surfaces must be clean, sound, dry and free from organic growth.	Solvent-based paint	Acrylic paint	Wood dye
SUITABLE TO COVER			
Softwoods	●	●	●
Hardwoods	●	●	●
Oily hardwoods	●	●	●
Planed wood	●	●	●
Sawn wood			
DRYING TIME: HOURS			
Touch-dry	4	1–2	0.5
Recoatable	16	4–6	6
THINNERS: SOLVENTS			
Water		●	●
White spirit	●		●
Methylated spirit			
Special thinner			
NUMBER OF COATS			
	1–2	1–2	2–3
COVERAGE			
Sq metres per litre	15–16	10–14	16–30
METHOD OF APPLICATION			
Brush	●	●	●
Paint pad	●	●	●
Cloth			●

such as how long the finishes take to dry, how many coats are necessary, which type of solvents should be used to thin them and what sort of coverage they provide.

FINISHES FOR WOODWORK							
Protective wood stain	Coloured preserver	Varnish	Acrylic varnish	Cold-cure lacquer	Oil	Wax polish	French polish
•	•	•	•	•	•	•	
•	•	•	•	•	•	•	•
•		•	•	•	•	•	•
•	•	•	•	•	•	•	•
	•						
0.5–4	1–2	2–4	0.5	1	1	–	0.5
4–16	2–4	14	2	2	6	1	24
•	•		•				
•	•	•			•	•	
							•
				•			
1–2	–	2–3	3	2–3	3	2	10–15
10–25	4–12	15–16	15–17	16–17	10–15	VARIABLE	VARIABLE
•	•	•	•				•
•	•						
		•	•		•	•	

PAINTING WOODWORK

Wood is a fibrous material with
a definite grain pattern and
different rates of absorption. And
some species contain knots that may
ooze resin. These are all qualities that have a bearing
on the type of paint you use when decorating as well
as the techniques and tools you need to apply it.

Basic application

It is essential to prepare and prime all new woodwork
before applying the finishing coats. If you're going to
use conventional solvent-based paint, apply 1 or 2
undercoats, depending on the covering power of the
paint. As each coat hardens, rub down with fine wet-
and-dry paper to remove blemishes, then wipe the
surface with a cloth dampened with white spirit.

   Apply the paint with vertical brushstrokes, and
then spread it sideways to even out the coverage.
Finish with light strokes (laying off) in the direction
of the grain. Blend the edges of the next application
while the paint is still wet. Don't go back over a
painted surface that has started to dry, or you will
leave brushmarks in the paintwork.

   For one-coat or acrylic paints simply lay on the
paint liberally with almost parallel strokes, then lay
off lightly. Blend wet edges quickly.

TIP: It is best to use 25 and 50 mm (1 and 2 in) paintbrushes, and a 12 mm (½ in) brush for narrow glazing bars.

REMOVING SPECKS AND BRISTLES

Don't try to remove brush bristles or specks of fluff from fresh paintwork once a skin has started to form. Let the paint harden, then rub down with wet-and-dry paper. The same applies if you discover runs.

PAINTING A PANEL

When painting up to the edge of a panel brush from the centre out – if you flex the bristles against the edge the paint will run. Mouldings also flex bristles unevenly, so take extra care at corners of moulded panels.

PAINTING SKIRTINGS

Use a simple plastic shield to protect the floor when painting skirting boards. Alternatively, cover the edges of fitted carpet with wide low-tack masking tape.

Painting skirtings.

PAINTING A STRAIGHT EDGE

To finish an area with a straight edge, use a small brush and place it a few millimetres from the edge. Flex the bristles and they will spread to lay an even coat.

PAINTING DOORS

Doors have a variety of faces and conflicting grain patterns, all of which need to be painted separately – yet the end result must look even in colour, with no ugly brushmarks or heavily painted edges. The recommended procedures for painting all types of doors are given on the following pages.

Preparation and basic technique

The first thing you should do is remove the door handles and wedge the door open so that it cannot be closed accidentally, locking you inside the room. You should, however, keep the handle in the room with you, just in case.

Aim to paint the door and its frame separately, so that there is less chance of you touching wet paintwork when passing through a freshly painted doorway. Paint the door first; and then when it's dry, you can finish the framework.

If you want to use a different colour for each side of the door, paint the hinged edge the colour of the closing face (the one that comes to rest against the frame). Paint the outer edge of the door the same colour as the opening face – this ensures there won't be any difference in colour when the door is viewed from either side. When painting the frame, each side should match the corresponding face of the door.

Paint the frame in the room into which the door swings – including the edge of the stop bead against which the door closes – to match the opening face. Paint the rest of the frame the colour of the closing face (*see* illustration below).

Painting each side of a door with a different colour

Work on the opening side first, painting the architrave (1) and doorframe (2) up to and including the edge of the doorstop one colour. Paint the face of the door and its opening edge (3) the same colour. Now paint the architrave and frame of the opposite side up to and over the doorstop (4) the second colour. Paint the opposite face of the door and its hinged edge (5) with the second colour.

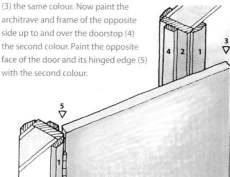

TIP: To paint a glazed door, you should start with the glazing bars and then simply follow the sequence that has been recommended for panelled doors (*see* p. 106).

Painting a flush door

To paint a flush door, start at the top and work down in sections, blending each one into the other. Lay on the paint, then finish each section with light vertical strokes. Finally, paint the edges, taking extra care to avoid paint runs.

Painting a panelled door

The different parts of a panelled door must be painted in a logical sequence. Finish each part with strokes running parallel to the direction of the grain.

Whatever style of panelled door you are painting, you should always start with the mouldings (1) followed by the panels (2). Paint the muntins (centre verticals) next (3), and then the cross rails (4). Finish the face by painting the stiles – the outer verticals (5). The last thing to paint then is the edge of the door (6).

Painting a panelled door.

PAINTING WINDOW FRAMES

Window frames also need to be painted in sequence so that the various components will be coated evenly (and also so you can close the windows at night). Clean the glass thoroughly before painting a window.

Painting a casement window

A casement window hinges like a door, so if you plan to paint each side a different colour, follow a similar procedure to that recommended for painting doors and frames. It's best to remove the stay and catch before painting – but so that you can still operate the window without touching wet paint, drive a nail into the underside of the bottom rail to act as a makeshift handle.

PAINTING SEQUENCE
First paint the glazing bars (1), cutting into the glass on both sides, then the top and bottom horizontal rails (2) followed by the vertical stiles (3). Paint the edges (4) then the frame (5).

Painting sequence for casement windows.

Window-painting tips

Here are a couple of invaluable tips that will help you when you are painting windows:

Keeping the window open while you work With the catch and stay removed, there's nothing to stop a casement window closing. Make a stay from a length of stiff wire.

Hook one end and slot it into one of the screw holes in the fixed frame, then wire the other end around a nail that you have driven into the underside of the window frame.

A temporary stay

Protecting the glass When painting the sides of wooden glazing bars, overlap the glass by about 2 mm ($^1/_{16}$ in) to prevent condensation or rain seeping between the glass and woodwork. If you find it difficult to achieve a satisfactory straight edge, use a plastic or metal paint shield, holding it against the edge of the frame, to protect the glass. Alternatively, run masking tape around the edges of the pane, leaving a slight gap so that the paint will seal the join between glass and frame. When the paint is touch-dry, peel off the tape. (Don't wait until the paint is completely dry or the film may peel off with the tape.) Scrape the glass with a sharp blade to remove paint spatters.

Painting a sash window

The following sequence describes the painting of a sash window from the inside. (To paint the outside face, use a similar procedure – but start with the lower sash.) If you are using different colours for each side, the demarcation lines are fairly obvious: when the window is shut, all the visible surfaces from one side should be the same.

PAINTING SEQUENCE

Raise the bottom sash and pull down the top one, so that you can paint the meeting rails.

Start by painting the bottom meeting rail of the top sash (1) and all the accessible parts of the vertical members (2). Reverse the position of the 2 sashes, leaving a gap top and bottom, in order to complete the painting of the top sash (3 – see p. 110).

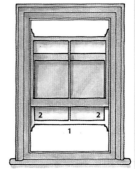

Raise the bottom sash and lower the top one.

Paint the bottom sash next (4), and then the window frame (5),

TIP: When you paint the runners make sure you only give them a very thin coat, to prevent the surfaces sticking.

except for the runners in which the sashes slide. Leave the paint to dry, then you can carry on by painting the inner runners (6) next, as well as a short section of the outer runners (7). As you work on the latter area, make sure that you pull the cords aside in order to avoid brushing paint on them – this would make them brittle and therefore significantly shorten their working lives.

Before the paint has time to dry, you should check that the sashes slide freely.

Reverse the position of the sashes.

Lower both sashes for access to the runners.

STAINING WITH WOOD DYES

Unless the wood is perfectly clean and free from grease, wood dye will be rejected, producing an uneven, patchy appearance. Strip any previous finish, and sand the wood with progressively finer abrasive papers. Always sand in the direction of the grain, as any scratches made across the grain will simply be emphasised by the dye.

Making a test strip

The final colour is affected by the nature of the timber, the number of coats, and the overlying clear finish. You can also mix compatible dyes to alter the colour, or dilute them with the appropriate thinner.

Start by making a test strip, so that you will have an accurate guide from which you can choose the depth of colour to suit the job in hand. Use a piece of timber from the same batch you are staining, or one that resembles it closely. Paint the strip with one coat of dye. Allow the dye to be absorbed, then apply a second coat, leaving a strip of the first application showing. It is rarely necessary to apply more than 2 coats of dye – but for the experiment add a third coat, and even a fourth, always leaving a strip of the previous application for comparison.

When the dye has dried completely, paint a band of clear varnish along the strip. Some polyurethane varnishes react unfavourably with oil-based dyes, so it is advisable to use only products that are made by the same manufacturer.

Working with wood dyes

When you wet a piece of timber, water is absorbed by the wood, raising a mass of tiny fibres across the surface. Applying a water-based dye does the same – which could potentially ruin the final finish. Avoid the problem by sanding the wood until it is perfectly smooth, then dampen the whole surface with a wet rag. Leave it to dry out, then sand the raised grain with very fine abrasive paper before you apply the dye. If you are going to be using an oil-based dye, this part of the process is unnecessary.

If you want to fill the grain, first apply a seal coat of clear finish over the dye. Choose a grain filler that matches the dye, adjusting the colour by adding a little dye to it. Make sure the dye and filler are compatible as an oil-based dye will not mix with a water-based filler, and vice versa; so check before you buy either.

Wood dye test strips

How to apply wood dye

Use a 100 mm (4 in) paintbrush to apply dyes over a wide, flat surface. Don't brush out a dye as you would paint, but apply it liberally and evenly, always in the direction of the grain. It is essential to blend the wet edges, so work fairly quickly. If you have applied a water-based dye with a brush, it is sometimes advantageous to wipe over the wet surface with a soft cloth to remove excess dye.

Using a paint pad is one of the most effective ways to achieve an even coverage. However, you may still need to use a brush for staining mouldings and to get the wood dye right into awkward corners. Because dyes are so fluid, it's often easier to apply them with a wad of soft lint-free rag, called a rubber. This will enable you to control runs on a vertical panel; it's also the best way to stain turned wood and rails (*see* below).

Working with a rubber

Wearing gloves, pour some dye into a shallow dish, saturate the rubber with dye, and then squeeze some out so that it is not dripping but is still wet enough to apply a liberal coat of dye to the surface.

Using a rubber.

STAINING PANELS, FLOORS AND DOORS

A wood dye can be a very effective way of finishing floors, doors and other areas in the home. The specific techniques for how to apply the dye are given below.

Staining a flat panel

Whenever possible, set up a panel horizontally for staining, either on trestles or raised on softwood blocks. Shake the container before use and pour the dye into a flat dish, so that you are able to load your applicator properly.

Brushes, pads and rubbers are all useful for applying wood dye to panels, floors and doors.

Apply the dye, working swiftly and evenly along the grain. Stain the edges at the same time as the top surface. The first application may have a slightly patchy appearance as it dries, because some parts of the wood will absorb more dye than others. (The second coat normally evens out the colour without difficulty.) If powdery deposits are left on the surface of the dry wood dye, wipe them off with a coarse, dry cloth, before applying the second coat.

Leave the dye to dry overnight, then proceed with the clear finish of your choice to seal the colourant.

Staining floors

Because a wooden floor is such a large area, it is more difficult to blend the wet edges of the dye. Work along 2 or 3 boards at a time, using a paint-brush and finishing at the edge of a board each time. Woodblock floors are even trickier; so work with an assistant, to cover the area quickly, blending and overlapping sections with a soft cloth.

Staining a door

So that it can be laid horizontally, stain a new or stripped door before it is hung. A flush door is stained like any other panel, but use a rubber (*see* p. 113) to colour the edges, so that wood dye does not run underneath and spoil the other side.

Pads for mouldings

It is relatively easy to apply a wood dye to a moulding using a narrow paintbrush. Alternatively, you could use a small paint pad that is usually intended for painting glazing bars.

HOW TO STAIN A PANELLED DOOR

When staining a panelled door, it is essential to follow a sequence that will allow you to pick up the wet edges before they dry.

Use a combination of paintbrush or paint pad and rubber to apply the dye evenly to the various parts of the door following the numbered sequence shown on the picture. Start with the inset panels (1), then continue by staining half of the vertical muntin (centre vertical) (2), the bottom cross rail (3) and then half the stiles (4). Pick up the wet edges with the other half of the muntin (5) and the stiles (6).

Stain the central cross rail (7), then repeat the procedure for the rest of the door (8–12). Unlike the order adopted when painting a panelled door, it is best not to stain the mouldings until the end (13), to prevent any overlapping showing on the flat surfaces. Stain the mouldings with a narrow brush and blend in the colour with a rubber.

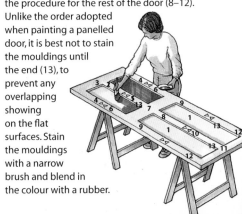

VARNISHING WOODWORK

Varnish serves two main purposes: to protect the wood from knocks, stains and other marks, and to give it a sheen that accentuates the grain pattern. Some varnishes can be used to change the colour of the wood to resemble another species or to give it a fresh, new look with a choice of bright colours.

The basic technique

You should apply varnish like paint, using a range of paintbrushes: you will find 12, 25 and 50 mm (½, 1 and 2 in) the most useful widths. For varnishing a floor, use a 100 mm (4 in) brush to achieve fast, even coverage.

Load a brush with varnish by dipping the first third of the bristles into the liquid, then touch off the excess on the inside of the container. Don't scrape the brush across the rim of the container – as that creates bubbles in the varnish, which can spoil the finish if transferred to the wood.

You can use a soft cloth pad, or rubber, to rub a sealer coat of varnish into the grain. Also, you'll find that a rubber is convenient for varnishing shaped or turned pieces of wood.

TIP: Always keep your brushes spotlessly clean; any remaining traces of paint on them may spoil the finish when you use them for varnishing.

Applying the varnish

Thin the first sealer coat of varnish by 10%, and rub it into the wood in the direction of the grain, using a cloth pad. Where a rubber is difficult to use, brush it on instead. Apply a second coat of varnish within the stipulated time. (If more than 24 hours have elapsed, lightly key the surface of solvent-based gloss varnish with fine abrasive paper and wipe the surface with a cloth dampened with white spirit to remove dust and grease – see right.) Apply a third coat if the surface is likely to take hard wear.

Using coloured varnish

Although wood stains can only be used on bare timber, you can use a coloured varnish to darken or alter the colour of woodwork that has been previously varnished, without having to strip the existing finish. Clean the surface with fine wire wool dipped in white spirit or a furniture cleaner that will remove old wax and dirt. Dry the surface with a clean cloth, then apply the varnish. (It may be worth making a test strip first to see how many coats you will need.)

Varnishing floors

Varnishing a floor is no different from varnishing any other woodwork; but due to the size of the area being treated in a confined space, solvent-based varnishes can produce an unpleasant concentration of fumes. Open all the windows and wear a respirator while you are working. Start in the corner furthest from the door and work back towards it. Brush the varnish out well, so that it does not collect in pools.

Dealing with dust particles

Minor imperfections and particles of dust stuck to the varnished surface can be rubbed down with fine abrasive paper between coats. If your top coat is to be a high-gloss finish, take even more care to ensure that your brush is perfectly clean.

If you are not satisfied with your final finish, wait until it is dry, then dip very fine wire wool in wax polish and rub the varnish with parallel strokes in the direction of the grain. Buff the surface with a soft duster.

Produce a soft sheen with wire wool and wax.

FINISHING METALWORK

Ferrous metals that are rusty will shed practically any paint film that is applied to them rapidly – so the most important aspect of finishing metalwork is thorough preparation and priming, in order to prevent the corrosion from returning. Applying the actual finish is the quickest part of the process.

Suitable finishes for metalwork

When you are choosing a finish for metalwork within the home, you need to make sure that it fulfils all your specific requirements. To help you with this, see the explanations below as well as the chart that is given on p. 123.

SOLVENT-BASED PAINTS
Conventional solvent-based paints are suitable for use on metal. Once it has been primed, interior metalwork will need at least one undercoat, plus a top coat.

METALLIC PAINTS
For a metallic-like finish, choose a paint that contains aluminium, copper, gold or bronze powder. These paints are all water-resistant and also able to withstand extremely high temperatures – up to about 100°C (212°F).

RADIATOR ENAMELS

Fast-drying water-based radiator enamel is supplied in a variety of colours designed to complement decorative colour schemes. A choice of satin and gloss finishes is available.

Radiator enamel can be applied to previously painted radiators, provided the surfaces are thoroughly cleaned and lightly sanded. Bare metal or factory primed radiators must be coated with a special compatible primer.

Turn off the heating and allow the radiators to cool, then apply the first coat of enamel, using a synthetic brush. Four hours later, apply a second coat.

You can coordinate your colour scheme by painting the skirting boards with the same paint.

BLACK LEAD

A cream used for cast ironwork, black lead is a mixture of graphite and waxes. It is reasonably moisture-resistant (*see* box, p. 122).

LACQUER

Virtually any clear lacquer can be used on polished metalwork without spoiling its appearance; however, many polyurethane lacquers have a tendency to yellow with age. For long-term protection of chrome plating, brass and copper, you should use a clear acrylic metal lacquer.

Methods of application

With the exception of black lead, you can use a paintbrush to apply the various metal finishes. In general, the techniques that are used are identical to those used for painting woodwork.

To prepare them for painting, you should remove metal door and window fittings, suspending them on wire hooks – which will help them to dry. Make sure that sharp edges are coated properly, as the finish can wear thin relatively quickly.

A roller is suitable for applying metal finishes to large flat surfaces while pipework requires the use of a special V-section roller, which is designed to coat curved surfaces.

Blacking cast iron

Black lead produces an attractive finish for cast iron. It is not a permanent or durable finish, and will have to be renewed periodically. It may transfer if rubbed hard.

Black lead comes in a tube similar to a toothpaste tube. Squeeze some of the cream onto a soft cloth and spread it onto the metal. Use an old toothbrush to scrub it into decorative ironwork. When you have covered the surface, buff it to a satin sheen with a dry cloth. Build up several applications to give a patina and a moisture-resistant finish.

This table provides at-a-glance information about the various metalwork finishes that have already been described on the previous pages.

The information includes details of what to apply the finish with, how many coats will be necessary and how long the finish will take to dry. Once you have chosen your required finish, this table will therefore provide you with the basic information you need before you apply it.

● Black dot denotes compatibility.
All surfaces must be clean, sound, dry and free from organic growth.

	FINISHES FOR METALWORK					
	Solvent-based paint	Metallic paint	Radiator enamel	Black lead	Lacquer	Bath paint
DRYING TIME: HOURS						
Touch-dry	4	4	0.5	–	0.25	6–10
Recoatable	14	8	4	–	–	16–24
THINNER: SOLVENTS						
Water			●			
White spirit	●	●		●		●
Cellulose thinners					●	
NUMBER OF COATS						
Normal conditions	1–2	1–2	2	VARIABLE	1	2
COVERAGE						
Sq metres of litre	12–16	10–14	15	VARIABLE	18	13–14
METHOD OF APPLICATION						
Brush	●	●	●	●	●	●
Paint pad	●					
Spray gun	●				●	
Cloth pad (rubber)				●		

Painting radiators and pipes

Leave radiators and hot-water pipes to cool before you paint them. Once you've chosen the correct paint, the only problem with decorating a radiator is how to paint the back: the best solution is to remove it completely or, if possible, to swing it away from the wall. After you have painted the back, you can then simply reposition the radiator and paint the front.

If this is inconvenient, use a special radiator roller or brush with a long handle. These are also ideal for painting in between the leaves of a double radiator. It is difficult to achieve a perfect finish – so aim at covering the areas that are on view when the radiator is in its final position.

You should never paint over radiator valves or fittings – otherwise, you won't be able to operate them afterwards. Also make sure you paint pipework lengthwise rather than across, or runs are likely to form. The first coat on metal piping will be streaky, so be prepared to apply 2 or 3 coats. Allow the paint to harden thoroughly before turning the heat back on.

Using a radiator brush on a double radiator.

Metal casement windows

Paint metal casement windows using the sequence that has already been described for wooden casements (*see* p. 107). This will allow you to close the window at night without spoiling a freshly painted surface.

Lacquering metalwork

Polish the metal to a high gloss, then use a nailbrush to scrub it with warm water containing some liquid detergent. Rinse the metal in clean water, then dry it thoroughly with an absorbent cloth.

Apply acrylic lacquer with a large, soft artist's paintbrush, working swiftly from the top. Let the lacquer flow naturally, and work all round the object to keep the wet edge moving. If you do leave a brushmark in partially set lacquer, finish the job and then warm the metal (by standing it on a radiator, if possible). As soon as the blemish disappears, remove the object from the heat and then allow it to cool back down gradually within a dust-free atmosphere.

You should use a large, soft artist's paintbrush to apply lacquer.

WALL- AND FLOORCOVERINGS

Quite apart from paint, there is a wide range of other coverings for walls and floors, including wood, ceramic tiles and wallpaper.

PANELLING

Walls that are in poor condition, except those that are damp, can be covered with panelling to conceal them and to provide a decorative surface. Panelling can be practical in other ways, too, when used in conjunction with insulation. There are two basic types of panelling for walls: solid-wood planking and wallboards faced with various decorative surfaces.

Tongue-and-groove boards

Solid-wood panelling is made from planks with a tongue along one edge and a matching groove on the other. The main function of this joint is to provide room for movement resulting from atmospheric changes, but it also allows for 'secret nailing' when fixing the planks to the wall.

The meeting edges of tongued, grooved and V-jointed (TGV) boards are machined to produce a decorative V-shaped profile, accentuating the junction between boards. Other types of tongue-and-groove boards have more-decorative profiles. Shiplap has a rebate on the back face, which holds down the coved front edge of the next board. Most boards are made from softwood, typically knotty pine.

TIP: Make sure you buy enough TGV boards to complete the work. Boards from another batch may not be compatible, because the machine used to shape their edge joints may have been set to slightly different tolerances.

Wallboards

Manufactured sheet wallboards are made to various standard sizes, and in thicknesses ranging from 4 to 6 mm ($^3/_{16}$ to $^1/_4$ in). Plywood or hardboard panels are faced with real-timber veneers or paper printed to simulate wood grain, and there are also plastic-faced boards available in a range of colours. Typical surfaces include V-grooving, embossed brick, stone, plaster and tiled effects.

Wall panels made from wood-fibre board are 12 mm ($^1/_2$ in) thick and can be bought with cork, grass and fabric surfaces to them. Such wall panels will reduce sound penetration and they are also heat-insulating.

Constructing a framework for panelling

If a wall is flat you can glue thick wallboards directly to the surface, but as most walls are uneven it is usually best to construct a frame from softwood battens, called furring strips. For TGV boarding and thin wallboards, this is the only practical solution. You can pin any type of panelling directly to the studs and noggings of a stud-partition wall.

To begin, prise off the skirting boards, picture rails and coving. If fixing to a solid wall, erect the framework using 50 x 25 mm (2 x 1 in) planed or sawn softwood. Treat the timber with wood preserver. You can reduce heat loss through an external wall by fitting insulation between the furring strips. Staple polythene sheeting over the strips to act as a vapour barrier. (It would then not be possible to glue boards to the framework.)

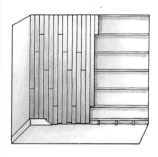

Wallboards Fix horizontal furring strips between the vertical strips that support the edges of panels.

The battens should be fixed 400 mm (1 ft 4 in) apart, using 50 mm (2 in) masonry nails or screws and wallplugs. Use a spirit level to align each batten with its neighbour. Pack out any hollows behind the furring strips using card. To fix wallboards, centre vertical furring strips on the edges of each wallboard. Fill in with horizontal strips every 400 mm (1 ft 4 in).

TGV boards can be arranged vertically, horizontally or diagonally. To fix vertical panelling, run the furring strips horizontally. The lowest strip should be level with the top of the skirting, with short vertical strips below it for attaching a length of skirting board. For horizontal boards, run the furring strips vertically. Nail offcuts to the bottom of the strips as spacers to support the skirting at the new level. Stagger the end joints between boards on alternate rows. You can fix diagonal boards to horizontal strips, staggering the joints between boards.

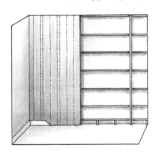

Vertical TGV panelling
Furring strips run horizontally across the wall.

ATTACHING STRIP PANELLING

Mark out and cut the boards to length, using a tenon saw, then sand the outer surfaces smooth before fixing them. Boards supplied as part of a kit may be supplied ready-sanded.

Fixing vertical panelling

With the grooved edge butted against the left-hand wall, plumb the first board with a spirit level. Nail it to the strips through the centre of its face, using 25 mm (1 in) panel pins. Use 36 mm (1½ in) pins when fixing to a stud-partition wall.

Slide the next board onto the tongue and, protecting the edge with a strip of wood, tap it in place with a hammer. Fix it to the battens using the secret-nailing technique – drive a pin at an angle through the inner corner of the tongue (1). Sink the head below the surface with a nail set. Slide on the next board to hide the fixings, and repeat the process to cover the wall (2). Use up short lengths of boarding by butting them end to end over a furring strip, but

1 Secret nailing

stagger such joints across the wall to avoid a continuous line. When you reach the other end of the wall, cut the last board down its length to fit the gap. Nail it through the face. If it's a tight fit, spring the last 2 boards in at the same time: slot the penultimate board's groove onto the exposed tongue, and then push both into position. Pin a small quadrant cover strip down the edges, nail the skirting in place and fit a ceiling coving to conceal the edges of the boards.

2 Fixing vertical TGV boards.

(labels in image: Fix boards tongue outwards / Horizontal Furrings / Skirting battens)

METAL CLIPS

Some pre-packed boards are attached to the battens with metal clips, which locate in the groove of a board leaving a tab that takes the pin. Plane the tongue from the first board and place that edge against the left-hand side wall. The clips are hidden by the next board.

Fixing horizontal panelling

Follow the same procedure described for vertical cladding, but position the first board just below skirting level, with its groove at the bottom.

Panelling around doors and windows

To panel around a door or window remove the architrave and sill mouldings and nail furring strips (1) up to the frame. Fix the panelling (2), and cover the edges with thin wooden strips (3). Refit the original mouldings (4) on top of the panelling.

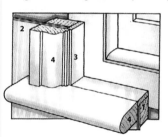

Panelling a ceiling

It is relatively straightforward to panel a ceiling with TGV boards, following the methods described for cladding a wall. First locate the joists, then nail or screw the furring strips across them.

Panelling adjacent walls

To panel adjacent walls, shape solid-wood strips to make neat internal or external corners.

1 Fit chamfered board in order to make an internal corner.

INTERNAL CORNERS
Where 2 boards meet in the corner, plane a chamfer along the edge of one board, then pin both boards through their faces to the furring strips (1). The detailing is similar for vertical and horizontal boards.

2 Joining vertical boards at an external corner.

EXTERNAL CORNERS
To join vertical boards, lap one with another and pin them together. Plane a chamfer on the outer corner (2). For horizontal boards, pin on a bevelled moulding to cover the end grain (3).

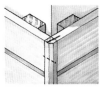

3 Joining horizontal boards at a corner.

ATTACHING SHEET PANELLING

Cut hardboard or plywood wallboards to size with a panel saw, making sure their face side is uppermost to avoid splitting the surface grain. Scribe the first board to the left-hand side wall and ceiling.

Pinning wallboards

Pin the panel to the furring strips, using a footlifter to hold it off the floor. If possible, hide the fixings by driving the pins through V-grooves running from top to bottom and tapping the pin heads just below the surface with a fine nail set, ready for filling later.

Butt-join the subsequent panels. The edges may be bevelled to make a matching V-groove. Cut the last board to fit against the opposite wall, then fit a cover strip and moulding.

Gluing wallboards

Wood-fibre boards can be pinned to the furring strips, but the nail heads may spoil the appearance. For a better result, use a proprietary all-purpose adhesive to glue the boards to the framework. If the panels are narrower than standard wallboards, then you will need to reduce the spacing of the furring strips accordingly.

When cutting wood-fibre panels, use a sharp knife rather than a saw, which tends to fray the edges. Fit the first board to the wall and ceiling. Follow the manufacturer's instructions for applying the glue. Some recommend applying it in patches or continuous bands, before pressing the panels in place. Strike the boards with the side of your fists to spread the glue.

You can also use the glue as a contact adhesive. To do this, apply the glue to the strips, press the board against them and then peel it off again, leaving glue on both surfaces. Wedge a batten under the bottom edge so that it will maintain its position relative to the wall (*see below*). When the glue is touch-dry, you can simply press the panel into place again and you will create an immediate bond.

Using contact adhesive Having peeled a board off the glued strips, wedge it against the ceiling until the adhesive is touch-dry.

CHOOSING WALLCOVERINGS

There are many different
coverings for walls with
various textures. As well as
the decorative statement
that can be made, you should
ensure the covering you
choose is suitable for your walls.

Preparing the surface

Although many wallcoverings will
cover minor blemishes, walls and ceilings
should be clean, sound and smooth. Eradicate damp
and organic growth before hanging any wallcovering.
Consider whether you should size the walls to reduce
paste absorption (see p. 44).

Coverings that camouflage

Although a poor surface should be repaired, some
coverings hide minor blemishes, as well as providing
a foundation for other finishes.

EXPANDED-POLYSTYRENE SHEET

This is a thin polystyrene sheet used for lining a wall
before papering. It reduces condensation and also
bridges hairline cracks and small holes. It dents easily,
so don't use it where it will take a lot of punishment.

LINING PAPER

This is a cheap buff-coloured wallpaper for lining uneven or impervious walls prior to hanging a heavy or expensive wallcovering. It also provides an even surface for emulsion paint.

WOODCHIP PAPER

Woodchip paper is made by sandwiching particles of wood between 2 layers of paper. It is inexpensive, easy to hang (but problematic to cut) and must be painted once hung.

RELIEF PAPERS

Wallpapers that have deeply embossed patterns are good at hiding minor imperfections. Reliefs are invariably painted, with emulsion, satin-finish oil paints or water-based acrylics.

Lincrusta, which was the first ever embossed wallcovering, consists of a solid film of linseed oil and fillers fused onto a backing paper before the pattern is applied with an engraved steel roller. It is still available, though many people prefer embossed-paper wallcoverings or the superior-quality versions made from cotton fibres.

Lightweight vinyl reliefs are also popular. During manufacture they are heated in an oven, which 'blows' or expands the vinyl, thereby creating deeply embossed patterns.

The choice of wallcoverings

Although wallcoverings are often called 'wallpaper', only a proportion of the wide range available is made solely from wood pulp.

WASHABLE PAPERS

These are printed papers with a thin impervious glaze of PVA, which creates a spongeable surface. Washables are suitable for bathrooms and kitchens. The surface must not be scrubbed, or the plastic coating will be worn away.

VINYL WALLCOVERINGS

A base paper, or cotton backing, is coated with a layer of vinyl upon which the design is printed. Heat is used to fuse the colours and vinyl. The result is a durable, washable wallcovering ideally suited to bathrooms and kitchens. Many vinyls are sold ready-pasted.

FOAMED-PLASTIC COVERING

This is a lightweight wallcovering made solely of foamed polyethylene, best used on walls not exposed to wear. You paste the wall instead of the covering.

FLOCK WALLCOVERINGS

Flock papers have the major pattern elements picked out with a fine pile produced by gluing synthetic or natural fibres to the backing paper; the pattern stands out in relief, with a velvet-like texture. Standard flock papers are difficult to hang, as contact with paste will ruin the pile. Vinyl flocks are less delicate and may even come ready-pasted.

GRASS CLOTH
Natural grasses are woven into a mat and glued to a paper backing. While these wallcoverings are very attractive, they are fragile and difficult to hang.

CORK-FACED PAPER
This is surfaced with thin sheets of coloured or natural cork. It is quite hardwearing.

PAPER-BACKED FABRICS
Finely woven cotton, linen or silk on a paper backing has to be applied to a flat surface. They are expensive and not easy to hang – avoid smearing the fabric with adhesive. Most fabrics are delicate, but some are plastic-coated.

UNBACKED FABRICS
Upholstery-width fabric can be wrapped around panels, which are then glued or pinned to a wall.

Estimating coverage

Calculating the number of rolls of wallcovering you need will depend mainly on the size of the roll – both the length and width. However, you also need to take

Walls: Standard rolls
Measure your room, then look down the height column and across the wall column to estimate the number of standard rolls needed.

MEASUREMENTS AROUND WALLS (including doors and windows)	HEIGHT OF ROOM IN METRES FROM SKIRTING							
	2–2.5 m	2.25–2.5 m	2.5–2.75 m	2.75–3 m	3–3.25 m	3.25–3.5 m	3.5–3.75 m	3.75–4 m
WALLS	**NUMBER OF ROLLS REQUIRED**							
10 m	5	5	6	6	7	7	8	8
10.5 m	5	6	6	7	7	8	8	9
11 m	5	6	7	7	8	8	9	9
11.5 m	6	6	7	7	8	8	9	9
12 m	6	6	7	8	8	9	9	10
12.5 m	6	7	7	8	9	9	10	10
13 m	6	7	8	8	9	10	10	10
13.5 m	7	7	8	9	9	10	10	11
14 m	7	7	8	9	10	10	11	11
14.5 m	7	8	8	9	10	10	11	12
15 m	7	8	9	9	10	11	12	12
15.5 m	7	8	9	9	11	11	12	13
16 m	8	8	9	10	11	11	12	13
16.5 m	8	9	9	10	11	12	13	13
17 m	8	9	10	10	11	12	13	14
17.5 m	8	9	10	11	12	13	14	14
18 m	9	9	10	11	12	13	14	15
18.5 m	9	10	11	11	12	13	14	15
19 m	9	10	11	12	13	14	15	16
19.5 m	9	10	11	12	13	14	15	16
20 m	9	10	11	12	13	14	15	16

into consideration the pattern repeat and make allowance for cutting around obstructions.

The width of a standard roll of wallcovering is 520 mm (1 ft 9 in), the length 10.05 m (33 ft). Use the chart provided here to estimate how many rolls you are likely to need for your walls.

	HEIGHT OF ROOM IN METRES FROM SKIRTING							
	2–2.5 m	2.25–2.5 m	2.5–2.75 m	2.75–3 m	3–3.25 m	3.25–3.5 m	3.5–3.75 m	3.75–4 m
WALLS	**NUMBER OF ROLLS REQUIRED**							
20.5 m	10	11	12	13	14	15	16	17
21 m	10	11	12	13	14	15	16	17
21.5 m	10	11	12	13	14	15	17	18
22 m	10	11	13	14	15	16	17	18
22.5 m	11	12	13	14	15	16	17	18
23 m	11	12	13	14	15	17	18	19
23.5 m	11	12	13	15	16	17	18	19
24 m	11	12	14	15	16	17	18	20
24.5 m	11	13	14	15	16	18	19	20
25 m	12	13	14	15	17	18	19	20
25.5 m	12	13	14	16	17	18	20	21
26 m	12	13	15	16	17	19	20	21
26.5 m	12	14	15	16	18	19	20	22
27 m	13	14	15	17	18	19	21	22
27.5 m	13	14	16	17	18	20	21	23
28 m	13	14	16	17	19	20	21	23
28.5 m	13	15	16	18	19	20	22	23
29 m	13	15	16	18	19	21	22	24
29.5 m	14	15	17	18	20	21	23	24
30 m	14	15	17	18	20	21	23	24

MEASUREMENTS AROUND WALLS

PASTING WALLCOVERINGS

You can use any wipe-clean table for pasting, but a narrow fold-up pasting table is a good investment if you are doing a lot of decorating. Lay several cut lengths of paper face down on the table to keep it clean. To stop the paper rolling up while you are pasting, tuck the ends under a length of string tied loosely round the table legs.

Applying the paste

Use a large, soft wall brush or pasting brush to apply the paste. Mix the paste in a plastic bucket and tie string across the rim to support the brush, keeping its handle clean while you hang the paper.

Align the wallcovering with the far edge of the table, to avoid brushing paste on the table – where it could be transferred to the face of the wallcovering. Apply the paste by brushing away from the centre. Paste the edges and remove any lumps.

Paste the second half of the covering then fold it to meet the other half.

TIP: Instead of pasting the back of exotic wallcoverings paste the wall, to reduce the risk of marking the delicate faces.

If you prefer, apply the paste with a short-pile paint roller. Pour the paste into a roller tray and roll it onto the wallcovering in one direction only, towards the end of the paper.

Pull the wallcovering to the front edge of the table and paste the other half. Fold the pasted end over – don't press it down – and slide the length along the table to expose an unpasted section.

Paste the other end (*see* left), then fold it over to almost meet the first cut end. The second fold is invariably deeper than the first – a handy way to tell which is the bottom of patterned wallcoverings. Fold long drops concertina-fashion.

Hang vinyls and lightweight papers immediately; drape other wallcoverings over a broom handle spanning 2 chair backs, or other supports, and leave to soak. Some very heavy or embossed wallcoverings need to soak for 15 minutes.

Ready-pasted wallcoverings
Many wallcoverings come pre-coated with adhesive, which is activated by soaking a cut length in a trough of cold water. Plastic troughs are sold for the purpose.

PAPERING WALLS

Don't apply a wallcovering of any kind until all the woodwork in the room has been painted or varnished, and the ceiling painted or papered.

Where to start

The traditional method for papering a room is to hang the first length next to a window close to a corner, then work in both directions away from the light. But you may find it easier to paper the longest uninterrupted wall first, so you get used to the basic techniques before tackling corners or obstructions.

If your wallcovering has a large regular motif, you can centre the first length over a fireplace for symmetry. You could also centre this first length between 2 windows – unless that means you will be left with narrow strips each side, in which case it's best to butt 2 lengths on the centre line.

Hanging paper on a straight wall

The walls of a room are rarely truly square, so use a plumb line to mark a vertical guide against which to hang the first length of wallcovering. Mark the line one roll-width away from a corner minus 12 mm ($\frac{1}{2}$ in), so the first length will overlap the adjacent wall.

Allowing enough length for trimming at the ceiling, unfold the top section of the pasted paper and hold it against the plumbed line. Brush the paper gently onto the wall, working from the centre out in order to get rid of trapped air. Draw the point of your scissors along the ceiling line, peel back the top edge and cut

Trim the paper at the ceiling.

along the crease. Smooth the paper back and tap it down with the brush. Unpeel the lower fold, smooth it onto the wall then tap it into the corner. Crease the bottom edge against the skirting, then trim in the same way. Hang the next length and slide it to align the pattern and produce a perfect butt joint. Wipe any paste from the surface with a damp cloth. Continue the process, ensuring the last drop overlaps the adjoining wall by 12 mm (½ in).

Papering round a corner

Turn the corner by marking another plumbed line so that the next length of paper covers the overlap from the first wall. If the piece you trimmed off at the

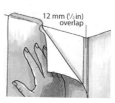

12 mm (½ in) overlap

As you paper round an internal corner cover the overlap from the first piece.

corner is wide enough, you can use it as your first length on the new wall.

If there's an alcove on both sides of a fireplace, wrap the paper around the external corners. Trim the last length to wrap round the corner, lapping the next wall by about 25 mm (1 in). Hang the remaining strip with its edge about 12 mm ($\frac{1}{2}$ in) from the corner.

Papering behind radiators

If you can't remove a radiator, turn off the heating and allow it to cool. Use a steel tape to measure the positions of the fixing brackets. Transfer those measurements to a length of wall-covering and slit it from the bottom to the top of the bracket. Feed the pasted paper behind the radiator and down both sides of the brackets. Use a seam roller to press it to the wall. Crease and trim to the skirting board.

Papering around doors and windows

When you get to the door, hang the length of paper next to the frame, brushing down the butt joint to align the pattern and allowing the other edge to loosely overlap the door. Make a diagonal cut in the excess towards the top corner of the frame. Crease the waste down the side of the frame with scissors, peel it back and trim off, then brush back. Leave a 12 mm ($\frac{1}{2}$ in) strip for turning on the top of the frame. Fill in with short strips above the door, then butt the next full length over the door and cut the excess diagonally into the frame, pasting the rest of the strip down the other side of the door. Cut off the waste.

Treat a flush window frame in a similar way. If the window is set into a reveal, hang the length of paper next to the window and allow it to overhang the opening. Make a horizontal cut just above the edge of the reveal. Make a similar cut near the bottom, then fold the paper around to cover the side of the reveal. Crease and trim along the frame and sill. To fill in the reveal, cut a strip of paper to match the width and pattern of the overhang above it. Paste this, slip it under the overhang and fold it around the top of the reveal. Cut through the overlap with a smooth wavy stroke, then remove the excess paper and roll down the joint. To continue, hang short lengths on the wall below and above the window, wrapping top lengths into the reveal.

To fill a window reveal cut and fold a strip of paper around the top of it.

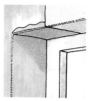

Cut through the piece of overlapping paper using a wavy stroke.

CHOOSING TILES

With an almost inexhaustible range of colours, textures and patterns to choose from, tiling is one of the most popular methods of decorating walls and floors.

Ceramic wall tiles

The majority of ceramic wall tiles are coated with a thick layer of glaze that makes them durable, waterproof and relatively easy to cut. Unglazed tiles are generally more subtle in colour, and may need to be sealed to prevent them absorbing grease and dirt.

Machine-made tiles are perfectly regular in shapes and colour, and are therefore simple to lay and match. With hand-made tiles, there is much more variation, but this irregularity merely adds to their appeal.

Although rectangular tiles are available, the majority of wall tiles are 100 or 150 mm (4 or 6 in) square. As well as a wide range of plain colours, you can buy printed and high-relief moulded tiles in both modern and traditional styles. Patterned tiles can be used for decorative friezes or individual inserts.

Ceramic wall tiles

Mosaic tiles

These are, in effect, small versions of standard ceramic tiles. To lay them individually would be time-consuming and lead to inaccuracy, so they are usually joined, either by

Mosaic tiles

a paper covering or a mesh backing, into larger panels. Because they are small, mosaics can be used on curved surfaces and they fit irregular shapes better than large ceramic tiles do.

Ceramic floor tiles

Floor tiles are larger and thicker than wall tiles, so that they can withstand the weight of furniture and foot traffic. As with wall tiling, square and rectangular tiles are the most economical ones to buy and lay, but hexagonal and octagonal floor tiles are also available. Choose non-slip ceramic tiles for bathrooms and other areas where the floor is likely to become wet.

Quarry tiles

Thick unglazed quarry tiles are ceramic tiles with a mellow appearance. The colours are limited to browns, reds, black and white. Hand-made quarries are uneven in colour, producing a beautiful mottled effect.

Quarry tiles

Round-edge 'bullnose' quarry tiles can be used as treads for steps; and shaped tiles are available for creating a skirting around a quarry-tile floor.

Stone and slate flooring

A floor laid with natural stone or slate tiles will be exquisite but expensive. Sizes and thicknesses vary according to the manufacturer – some will even cut to measure. These materials are so costly that you should consider hiring a professional to lay them.

Stone and slate floor tiles

Carpet tiles

These tiles have advantages over wall-to-wall carpeting. For example, an error is less crucial when cutting a single tile to fit; and, being loose-laid, worn, burnt or stained tiles can be replaced instantly. However, you can't substitute a brand-new tile several years later, because the colour simply won't match. Therefore, it's worth buying several spares initially and swapping them around regularly to even out the wear and colour change. Most types of carpet are also available as tiles, including cord, loop and twist piles, both in wool and a range of man-made fibres.

Carpet tiles come mostly in plain colours or with small patterns. Some tiles have an integral rubber underlay on the underside.

Vinyl tiles

Vinyl can be cut easily; and provided the tiles are firmly glued with good butt joints between them, the floor will be waterproof. They are also among the cheapest and easiest floor coverings to lay.

A standard coated tile has a printed pattern sandwiched between a vinyl backing and a harder, clear-vinyl surface. Solid-vinyl tiles are made entirely of the hardwearing plastic. Some vinyl tiles have a high proportion of mineral filler so are stiff and must be laid on a perfectly flat base. Unlike standard vinyl tiles, they will resist some rising damp in a concrete subfloor. Most tiles are square or rectangular, but there are interlocking shapes and hexagons. There are also many patterns and colours to choose from.

Vinyl tiles can simulate other flooring materials.

Polystyrene tiles

Although expanded-polystyrene tiles will not significantly reduce heat loss from a room, they are able to prevent condensation and mask a ceiling that is in poor condition. Polystyrene cuts easily, provided the trimming knife is very sharp. For safety in case of fire, choose a self-extinguishing type and do not overpaint with an oil paint. Polystyrene wall tiles are available, but they crush easily and are not suitable for use in a vulnerable area. The tiles may be flat or decoratively embossed.

Polystyrene
tiles

Rubber tiles

These were originally made for use in business premises such as shops and offices. However, being hardwearing yet soft and quiet to walk on, they also make ideal domestic floorcoverings and they have become quite popular in recent years. Rubber tiles are usually studded or textured to improve the grip.

Mirror tiles

Square and rectangular mirror tiles are attached to walls by means of a self-adhesive pad in each corner. Both silver and bronze finishes are available.

Plastic tiles

Insulated plastic wall tiles inhibit condensation. Provided you don't use abrasive cleaners on them, they are relatively durable; but they will melt if they are subjected to direct heat. A special grout is applied to fill the 'joints' that are moulded across the 300 mm (1 ft) square tiles.

Plastic tiles

Cork tiles

Cork is a popular covering for walls and floors. It is easy to lay with contact adhesive, and can be cut to size and shape with a knife. A wide choice of textures and warm colours is available. Pre-sanded but unfinished cork will darken in tone when you varnish it. You can also buy ready-finished tiles with plastic and wax coatings.

Cork tiles

SETTING OUT WALL TILES

Having prepared the wall surfaces (*see* pp 44–8), you must measure each wall to determine where to start tiling and how to avoid making too many awkward cuts. The best way is to mark a row of tiles on a straight wooden batten, which you can use as a gauge stick.

Setting out for tiling

Plan different arrangements of wall tiles as shown below. Start by temporarily fixing a horizontal batten at the base of the field (1). Mark the centre of the wall (2), gauge from the mark then fix a vertical batten to indicate the side of the field (3). You should start under a dado rail with whole tiles (4) and also use whole tiles at sill level (5). Place cut tiles at the back of a reveal (6) and support tiles over a window while they set (7).

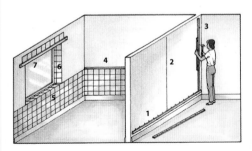

CUTTING CERAMIC TILES

For any but the simplest of tiling projects, you will have to cut the tiles to fit around obstructions and to fill the narrow margins around a main field of tiles. Glazed tiles are relatively easy to cut, because they snap readily along a line scored in the glaze. Cutting unglazed tiles can be a lot trickier. Whatever method you adopt, protect your eyes with safety spectacles or goggles when cutting ceramic tiles.

Making straight cuts

It is possible to scribe and snap thin ceramic tiles using little more than a basic tile scorer and a metal ruler, but the job is made a lot easier if you use a tile-cutting jig.

You can buy inexpensive plastic jigs that are used to guide a hand-held scorer, then snap the tile with a special pincer-action tool (*see* right). However, if you anticipate having to cut a lot of tiles, or ones that are relatively thick, you should invest in a sturdy lever-action jig. A good-quality jig will be

Use a special tool that has a pincer action to snap the tile.

fitted with a tungsten-carbide cutting wheel and angled jaws that will snap most sorts of tiles effortlessly.

To use such a jig, you should mark each end of the line on the face of a glazed tile with a felt-tip pen (use a pencil on unglazed tiles), then place the tile against the jig's fence, aligning the marks with the cutting wheel. Then, with one smooth stroke, push the wheel across the surface in order to score the glaze (1).

1 Score the marked line using one smooth stroke.

Next place the tile in the jig's snapping jaws, making sure that you align the scored line with the arrow that is marked on the tool. Then simply press down on the lever to snap the tile (2).

2 Snap the tile by pressing down on the lever.

FIXING CERAMIC WALL TILES

Start by tiling the main areas with whole tiles, leaving the narrow gaps around the edges to be filled with cut tiles later. This will allow you to work relatively quickly and to check the accuracy of your setting out before you have to make any tricky cuts.

Choosing tile adhesive and grout

Ceramic tiles are stuck to the wall with special adhesives that are generally sold ready-mixed, although a few need to be mixed to a paste with water. The tubs or packets will state the coverage you can expect.

Grout is a similar material that is used to fill the gaps between the tiles. Unless you have specific requirements, it is convenient to use one of the many adhesives that can be used for both jobs.

Most tile adhesives and grouts are water-resistant, but you should check that any material you use for tiling shower surrounds is completely waterproof and can be subjected to the powerful spray generated by a modern shower. If tiles are to be laid on a wallboard, make sure you use a flexible adhesive. Heat-resistant adhesive and grout may be required in the vicinity of a cooker and around a fireplace. You should use an epoxy-based grout for worktops to keep them germ-free.

Applying whole tiles

A serrated plastic spreader is normally supplied with each tub of adhesive, but if you are tiling a relatively large area it pays to buy a notched metal trowel for applying the adhesive to the wall.

Use the straight edge of the spreader or trowel to spread enough adhesive to cover about 1 m (3 ft) square; then turn the tool around and drag the notched edge through the adhesive so that it forms horizontal ridges.

Press the first tile into the angle formed by the setting-out battens. Press the next tile into place with a slight twist until it is firmly fixed, using plastic spacers to form the grout lines between the tiles. Lay additional tiles to build up 3 or 4 rows at a time, then wipe any adhesive from the surface of the tiles, using a clean damp sponge.
Spread more adhesive, and continue to tile along the batten until the first rows of whole tiles are complete. From time to time, check that your tiling is accurate by holding a batten and spirit level across the

Stick the first tile against the setting-out battens.

faces and along the top and side edges. When you
have completed the entire field, scrape adhesive
from the margins and allow the rest to set firm before
removing the setting-out battens.

Marking and fitting margin tiles

It is necessary to cut tiles one at a time to fit the
gaps between the field tiles and the adjacent walls:
because walls are never truly square, the margins
are bound to be uneven. Mark each margin tile by
placing it face down over its neighbour with one
edge against the adjacent wall (1); make an allowance
for the normal spacing between the tiles. Transfer
the marks to the edges of the tile using a felt-tip
pen. Having cut it to size (*see* pp 155–6), spread
adhesive onto the back of each tile (2) and press
them into the margin.

1 Mark the back of
a margin tile.

2 Butter adhesive onto
the back of a cut tile.

TIP: You can use your gauge stick to check how the tiles will fit around socket outlets, light switches, pipes and other obstructions. Make slight adjustments to the position of the main field in order to avoid difficult shaping around these.

Grouting the tiles

Standard grouts are those in white, grey or brown, but coloured grouts are also available, or you can mix coloured pigments with dry powdered grout.

Leave the tile adhesive to harden for 24 hours, then use a rubber-bladed spreader or a tiler's rubber float to press grout into the joints. Spread it in all directions to make sure every joint is well filled.

Using a barely damp sponge, wipe grout from the surface before it sets. Sponging alone is sufficient to finish the joints, but compressing each joint helps to guarantee a waterproof seal; do this by running the end of a blunt stick along each joint. When the grout has dried, you should polish the tiles with a dry cloth.

To make sure the grout hardens thoroughly, don't use a newly tiled shower for about 7 days.

Press grout into the joints with a spreader.

FIXING OTHER WALL TILES

Ceramic tiles are ideal in bathrooms and kitchens but in other areas you may decide to use tiles for reasons other than practicality. Here are some guidelines on how to fix other types of tiles.

Mosaic tiles

When applying mosaic tiles to a wall, use adhesives and grouts similar to those recommended for standard ceramic tiles. Some mosaics have a mesh backing, which is pressed into the adhesive. Others have facing paper, which is left on until the adhesive sets.

Mirror tiles

Mirror tiles are usually fixed close-butted with self-adhesive pads. No grouting is necessary.

Plastic tiles

To fix plastic tiles you will need to use special adhesive supplied by the manufacturer. Grout the moulded 'joints' with the branded non-abrasive product sold with the tiles.

Cork tiles

Use a rubber-based contact adhesive to fix cork tiles. If any gets onto the face of a tile, clean it off immediately with the recommended solvent on a cloth.

SETTING OUT SOFT FLOOR TILES

Soft tiles – such as vinyl, rubber, cork and carpet –
are relatively large, so you can cover the floor fairly
quickly. Also, they can be cut easily, with a sharp
trimming knife or even with scissors, so fitting to
irregular shapes isn't difficult at all.

Marking out the floor

It is possible to lay soft tiles onto either a solid-
concrete or a suspended wooden floor, provided the
surface is level, clean and dry. Most soft tiles are set
out in a similar way: find the centre of 2 opposite
walls, and snap a chalked string between them to
mark a line across the floor (1). Lay loose tiles at right
angles to the line up to one wall. If there's a gap of
less than half a tile-width, move the line sideways by
half a tile in order to create a wider margin.

To draw a line at right angles to the first, using
string and a pencil as an improvised compass, scribe
arcs on the marked line at equal distances each side
of the centre (2).

From each point, scribe arcs on both sides of the
line (3) that bisect each other. Join the points to form
a line across the room. As before, lay tiles at right
angles to the new line to make sure margin tiles are
at least half-width. Nail a guide batten against one
line, to help align the first row of tiles.

Setting out A quartered room ensures that the tiles are laid symmetrically. This method is suitable for vinyl, rubber, cork and carpet tiles.

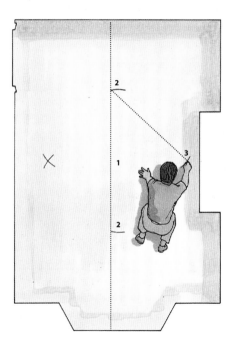

Setting out floors for diagonal tiling

Arranging tiles diagonally can create an unusual decorative effect, especially if your choice of tiles enables you to mix colours. Setting out and laying the tiles off centre is not complicated – it's virtually the same as fixing them at right angles; the only difference is that you will be working towards a corner instead of a straight wall.

Mark a centre line, and bisect it at right angles, using an improvised compass as before. Next, draw a line at 45° through the centre point. Dry-lay a row of tiles to plot the margins, and mark another line at right angles to the first diagonal. Check the margins as before. Fix a batten along one diagonal, which will act as a guide to laying the first row of tiles.

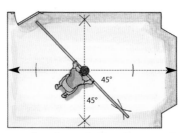

Setting out a floor diagonally Bisect the quartered room at 45°.

LAYING VINYL FLOOR TILES

Tiles pre-coated with adhesive can be laid quickly and simply, and there is no risk of squeezing glue onto the surface. If you are not using self-adhesive tiles, follow the tile manufacturer's instructions concerning the type of adhesive to use.

Fixing self-adhesive tiles

Stack the tiles in the room for 24 hours before you lay them, so they become properly acclimatised.

If the tiles have a directional pattern, make sure you lay them the correct way; some tiles have arrows printed on the back to guide you. Remove the protective paper backing from the first tile, then press its edge against the guide batten, aligning one corner

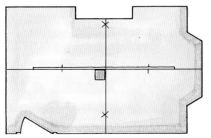

1 Place the first tile in angle of intersecting lines.

with the centre line (1). Gradually lower the tile onto the floor and press it down. Lay the next tile on the other side of the line, butting against the first tile (2). Form a square with two more tiles. Lay tiles around the square to form a pyramid (3). Continue in this way to fill one half of the room, then remove the batten and use the same technique to tile the other half.

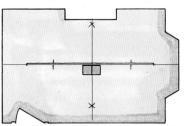

2 Butt up the next tile on the other side of the line.

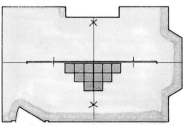

3 Lay tiles in a pyramid, then complete half room.

Finishing off the floor

As soon as you have laid all the floor tiles, wash over the surface with a damp cloth to remove any finger-marks. It's not often necessary to polish vinyl tiles, but you can apply an emulsion floor polish if you wish.

Fit a flat metal threshold bar (available from carpet suppliers) over the edge of the tiles when you finish at a doorway. When the tiles butt up to an area of carpet, fit a single threshold bar to the edge of the carpeting.

Lifting an old vinyl tile

Remove a damaged tile by chopping it out from the centre with a chisel. If the glue is firm warm the tile with an iron, using a piece of kitchen foil to keep the sole clean. Scrape the old glue from the floor, and stick the new tile in place. Place a heavy weight on top overnight.

Use an iron and kitchen foil to shift firm glue.

Trimming margin tiles

Floors are usually out of square, so you have to cut margin tiles to fit the gaps next to the skirting. To do this, lay a loose tile exactly on top of the last full tile.

Place another tile on top, with its edge touching the wall. Draw along the edge of this tile with a pencil to mark the tile below. Cut along the line, then glue the cut-off portion of the tile into the margin.

Cutting irregular shapes

To fit curves and mouldings, make a template for each tile out of thin card. Cut 'fingers' that can be pressed against the object to reproduce its shape, then transfer this to a tile.

Make a template out of thin card.

Fitting around pipes

Mark the position of the pipe on the tile with a compass. Starting from the perimeter of the circle, draw 2 parallel lines to the edge of the tile. Cut the hole for the pipe, using a home-made punch made out of a sharpened pipe offcut (place one end on the circle and hit the other end with a hammer). Finally cut a slit between the marked lines and fold the tile back to slide it into place.

Fold the tile back.

LAYING OTHER SOFT FLOOR TILES

The procedures for laying floor tiles made from carpet, cork and rubber are similar in many respects to those described for vinyl tiles. The differences are outlined below.

Carpet tiles

Carpet tiles are laid in the same way as vinyl tiles, except that they are not usually glued down. Set out centre lines on the floor, but don't fit a guide batten – simply aligning the row of tiles with the marked lines is sufficient.

Carpet tiles have a pile that has to be laid in the correct direction. This is sometimes indicated by arrows marked on the back of each tile.

Some tiles have ridges of rubber on the back, so they will slip easily in one direction but not in another. The non-slip direction is also typically denoted by an arrow on the back of the tile. It is usual to lay these tiles in pairs, so one prevents the other from moving. In any case, stick down every third row of tiles using double-sided

Checking the direction of the pile.

carpet tape, and tape all squares in areas where there is likely to be heavy traffic. (You can cut and fit carpet tiles in the same way described for vinyl tiles.)

Cork tiles

Use a contact adhesive when laying cork tiles: thixotropic adhesives allow a degree of movement as you position them. Make sure the tiles are level by tapping down the edges with a block of wood.

Tap the edges to level.

Unfinished tiles can be sanded lightly to remove minor irregularities. Vacuum then seal unfinished tiles, applying 2 or 3 coats of clear varnish.

Rubber tiles

You should bed rubber floor tiles onto latex flooring adhesive. To do this, place one edge and corner of each tile up against its neighbouring tiles before lowering it down gently onto the adhesive.

Lay rubber tiles on a bed of latex adhesive.

LAYING CERAMIC FLOOR TILES

Ceramic floor tiles are extremely durable and are
laid using a similar method to that described for
hanging ceramic tiles on a wall (*see* p. 157). However,
as they are usually thicker they are more difficult to
cut so it is best to take your time when setting out
the tiles, making any adjustments before cutting.

Setting out for tiling

Mark out the floor as for soft floor tiles, then set out the
field with battens. Fix temporary guide battens at the
edge of the field on the 2 adjacent walls farthest from
the door (1). Make sure that the battens are at true right
angles by measuring the diagonal (2) then dry-lay a
square of 16 tiles in the corner as a final check (3).

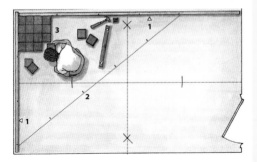

Laying the tiles

Use a floor-tile adhesive that is waterproof and slightly flexible when set. Spread it on with a notched trowel following the manufacturer's instructions. Spread enough adhesive on the floor to cover about 1 sq m (1 sq yd). Press the tiles into the adhesive, starting in the corner. Work along both battens and then fill in between to form the square, using plastic floor-tile spacers to create regular joints.

Wipe adhesive off the surface of the tiles with a damp sponge. Check their alignment with a straightedge, and ensure they are lying flat using a spirit level. Work your way along the whole length of 1 batten, laying a small square of tiles at a time; and then tile the rest of the floor in the same way, working back towards the door. Don't forget to scrape adhesive from the margins as you go.

Leave the adhesive to dry for 24 hours before walking on them, then remove the guide battens and fit the margin tiles.

Cutting ceramic floor tiles

Measure the margin tiles as described for wall tiles, then score and snap them with a tile-cutting jig. Because they are thicker, floor tiles will not snap quite so easily as wall tiles. Seal around the edge of the floor with a dark-coloured flexible sealant.

LAYING QUARRY TILES

Being tough and hardwearing, quarry tiles are an ideal choice for floors that receive heavy use. However, they are relatively thick and making even a straight cut requires a powered wet saw rather than a jig – so use quarry tiles only in areas that do not require a lot of complex shaping.

Do not lay quarry tiles on a suspended wooden floor: replace the floorboards with 18 or 22 mm (¾ or ⅞ in) exterior-grade plywood to provide a sufficiently flat and rigid base. A concrete floor presents no problems, so long as it is free from damp. You can lay quarries using a floor-tile adhesive, but the traditional method of laying the tiles on a bed of mortar takes care of slightly uneven floor surfaces.

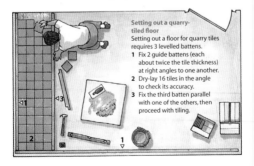

Setting out a quarry-tiled floor
Setting out a floor for quarry tiles requires 3 levelled battens.
1 Fix 2 guide battens (each about twice the tile thickness) at right angles to one another.
2 Dry-lay 16 tiles in the angle to check its accuracy.
3 Fix the third batten parallel with one of the others, then proceed with tiling.

Laying the tiles

Lay quarry tiles on a bed of mortar made from 1 part cement to 3 parts builder's sand. Soak the tiles in water prior to laying to prevent them absorbing water from the mortar too rapidly, which causes poor adhesion. Cut a stout board to span the parallel battens: this will be used to level the mortar bed and tiles. Cut a notch in each end to fit between the battens (1); its depth should match the thickness of a tile less 3 mm (⅛ in).

Spread the mortar to a depth of about 12 mm (½ in) to cover the area of 16 tiles. Level the mortar by dragging the notched side of the board across it (2). Dust

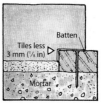

1 Cut notches in the levelling board.

2 Drag the board to level the mortar.

3 Cut margin tiles with a powered wet saw.

dry cement on the mortar, then lay the tiles along 3 sides of the square against the battens. Fill in the square, spacing the tiles by adjusting them with a trowel. Tamp down the tiles gently with the unnotched side of the board until they are level with the

Period effect You can recreate Victorian-style floors with modern quarry tiles.

battens. If the mortar is too stiff, brush water into the joints. Wipe any mortar from the tiles.

Fill in between the battens, then move one batten back to form another bay. Level it to match the first section. Tile section-by-section until the main floor area is complete. When it is firm enough to walk on, lift the battens and fill the margin with cut tiles (3).

Grouting quarry tiles

Push grout into the joints with a pointing trowel, and compress the grout with a blunted stick or a bricklayer's jointer. Keep the tiles as clean as possible, wiping excess grout off the surface with a damp sponge. When the grout has set, brush the floor clean.

PARQUET FLOORING

Parquet flooring is a relatively thin covering of decorative timber that is laid in the form of panels or narrow strips. Hardwoods such as oak, birch and cherry are used for their attractive grain patterns and rich colouring, which can be further highlighted by applying floor wax, polish or varnish.

Types of parquet flooring

Laying any type of parquet is as easy as tiling a floor, but you will need to take into consideration the nature of the subfloor.

STRIP FLOORING

Wood floors can be constructed from tongue-and-groove (T&G) or square-edged strips or tiles, either machined from solid timber or made from veneered plywood. They can be nailed to a wooden floor, or left as floating parquetry by gluing just the jointed edges together. Tiles and strips range in thickness from 9 to 18 mm (³/₈ to ³/₄ in). Fix them either as parallel strips or arrange them in order to create patterns.

HARDWOOD PANELS

Perhaps the most common form of hardwood flooring consists of panels 450 mm (1 ft 6 in) square made by gluing 8 mm (³/₈ in) solid-wood fingers into herringbone or basket-weave patterns. The panels are pre-sanded, and sometimes pre-finished as well. Some have a bitumen-impregnated backing to protect them from rising damp (although the floor itself must include a damp-proof membrane). Hardwood panels can be glued to wooden or concrete floors, their edges butted like floor tiles; some are self-adhesive.

TIMBER-FACED CORK

This is not a conventional parquet flooring, but consists of composite tiles made from a layer of cork backed with vinyl and surfaced with a natural or stained hardwood veneer. The timber is protected by a clear-vinyl coating. The tiles are available in 900 x 150 mm (3 ft x 6 in) strips. For setting out, fitting and cutting timber-faced cork, see the section on vinyl and cork tiles (see pp 165–70).

Hardwood parquet panels (left) and timber-faced cork (right)

Preparing the subfloor

Whether the subfloor is made of concrete or wood, it must be clean, dry and flat before parquet flooring is laid on top of it. You should use hardboard panels to level a wooden floor but screed a concrete base. Some manufacturers recommend that a building paper or thin plastic-foam underlay is laid for floating parquetry. To reduce the risk of warping, leave parquet panels or strips for several days in the room where they will be laid, so that they can adjust to the atmosphere.

PREPARING SOLID FLOORS

When laying parquet flooring on a solid-concrete base, ensure that the floor is completely dry and damp-proof (i.e. impervious to rising damp). Make good any defects, and then screed the surface with a proprietary self-levelling compound.

Preparing a solid floor Once you have made good any defects, screed the floor with self-levelling compound.

LAYING PANEL AND STRIP FLOORS

Other wooden floors include hardwood panels and strips of wood. These are also very straightforward to set out and lay.

Laying hardwood panels

Set out the flooring to calculate the position of the panels, as described for vinyl tiles (1); but instead of fixing a guide batten to the floor, stretch a length of string between nails that mark the edge of the last row of whole panels next to the wall farthest from the door (2).

Using a notched trowel, spread some of the recommended adhesive onto the subfloor so you can lay a row of panels next to the string. Align the first row with the string, levelling them with a softwood block and hammer (3). Check the alignment with a straightedge; then lay subsequent panels butted against the preceding row, working

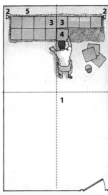

Fitting panels.

from the centre in both directions (4 – *see* p. 179).
Check alignment with a spirit level as you work.
Measure and mark margin panels as described for
vinyl tiles, but deduct 12 mm (½ in) to provide an
expansion gap. Cut and glue the panels in place (5).
Cover the gap with quadrant moulding.

How strips are fixed

Flooring strips are fixed across the floor, working away
from the skirting. Decide on the direction of the strips
then snap a chalked string parallel with the skirting (1).
Place the grooved edge of the first strip against the line,
then nail it through its face
with panel pins (2). Slot on
subsequent strips, and nail
through the tongues every
200 mm (8 in) up to 35 mm
(1½ in) from the ends (3).
(Drive the nails below the
surface for a neat finish.)
Stagger the end-to-end
joints as you work across
the floor (4). Make sure the
strips are cut 12 mm (½ in)
short of the skirting board.
Once all the boards are
laid, nail a cover moulding
all around the perimeter.

Fixing flooring strips.

CHOOSING CARPET

When shopping for carpeting there are various factors to consider, including fibre content, type of pile and durability.

Fibre content

The best carpets are made from wool or a mixture of wool plus a percentage of man-made fibre. Wool carpets are expensive, so manufacturers have experimented with a variety of fibres to produce cheaper but durable and attractive carpets. Materials such as nylon, polypropylene, acrylic, rayon and polyester are all used for carpet making.

Synthetic-fibre carpets were once inferior substitutes, often with unattractive shiny pile and a reputation for building up a charge of static electricity that produced mild shocks when anyone touched a metal door knob. Nowadays, manufacturers have largely solved the problem of static, but you should still seek the advice of the supplier before you buy.

As far as appearance is concerned, a modern carpet made from good-quality blended fibres is hard to distinguish from a wool one. Certain combinations produce carpets that are so stain-resistant they virtually shrug off spilled liquids. However, synthetic fibres tend to react badly to burns, shrivelling rapidly from the heat, whereas wool tends only to smoulder.

Which type of pile?

The nature of the pile is even more important to the feel and appearance of a carpet than the fibre content. Piled carpets are either woven or tufted. With woven carpets the pile is weaved simultaneously with the foundation, so that the strands are wrapped around and through the warp and weft threads. With tufted carpets, continuous strands are pushed between the threads of a pre-woven foundation. Although secured with an adhesive backing, tufted pile isn't as permanent as a woven pile. The various ways tufted and woven piles are created are described here.

1 Looped pile Ordinary looped pile provides a smooth feel.

2 Twisted pile Looped pile twisted for a coarser texture.

3 Cord pile Loops pulled tight against the foundation.

4 Cut pile Loops are cut, giving a velvety texture pile.

5 Velvet pile Loops are cut short for a close-stranded pile.

6 Saxony pile A long cut pile, up to 35 mm (1½ in).

The importance of underlay

A carpet benefits from a resilient cushion laid between it and the floor – it is more comfortable to walk on and the carpet lasts longer. Without this, dust may emerge from the divisions between the floorboards and begin to show as dirty lines. Underlay can be either a thick felt or a layer of foamed rubber or plastic.

Choosing a durable carpet

To be durable a carpet must have a dense pile. (When you fold the carpet and part the pile, you should not be able to see the backing.) The British Carpet Classification Scheme categorises floorcoverings according to their ability to withstand wear. If this is not stated on a carpet, ask the supplier how it is categorised.

DURABILITY RATING

CLASSIFICATION	APPLICATION
Light domestic	Bedrooms
Medium domestic	Light traffic only – dining room, well-used bedroom
General domestic	Living rooms
Heavy domestic	Hallways/stairs

TIP: The only special tool required for laying carpet is a knee kicker, for stretching it. This has a toothed head that is pressed into the carpet while you nudge the end with your knee.

LAYING CARPET

Carpet can be loose-laid, but a properly stretched and fixed carpet looks much neater and isn't actually that difficult to accomplish.

Methods of fixing

There are different methods for holding a carpet firmly in place, depending on the type.

CARPET TACKS

A 50 mm (2 in) strip can be folded under along each edge of the carpet, and nailed to a wooden floor with tacks about every 200 mm (8 in). (Lay the underlay 50 mm (2 in) short of the skirting to allow the carpet to lie flat along the edge.)

DOUBLE-SIDED TAPE

Use adhesive tape for rubber-backed carpets only. Stick 50 mm (2 in) tape around the perimeter of the room, then peel off the protective paper layer.

GRIPPER STRIPS

These wooden or metal strips have fine metal teeth that grip the woven foundation. Nail the strips to the floor, 6 mm (1/4 in) from the skirting, with the teeth pointing towards the wall. (Glue them to a concrete floor.) Cut underlay up to the edge of each strip.

Laying standard-width carpet

If you are laying separate underlay, join neighbouring sections with short strips of carpet tape or secure them with a few tacks. Roll out the carpet, butting one machine-cut edge against a wall: fix that to the floor. A pattern should run parallel to the main axis of the room. Stretch the carpet to the wall directly opposite and temporarily fix it with tacks, or slip it onto gripper strips. Don't cut the carpet yet.

Work from the centre towards each corner, stretching and fixing the carpet; then do the same at the other sides of the room. Cut a triangular notch at each corner, so the carpet lies flat. Adjust the carpet until it is stretched evenly, then fix it. When using tape or gripper strips, press the carpet into the angle between the skirting and the floor with a bolster chisel; then trim with a knife held at 45° to the skirting. Tuck the cut edge behind a gripper strip.

Cutting and joining carpet

Cut and fit carpet into doorways and around obstacles by pressing it up against the object, folding the waste back and trimming it off. Join carpets at a doorway with a threshold bar. Glue straight seams with latex adhesive or, for rubber-backed carpet, adhesive tape. Don't join expensive woven carpets: they should always be sewn by a professional.

Carpeting a staircase

Try to use standard-width narrow carpet on a staircase and cut underlay into separate pads for each tread.

CARPETING A STRAIGHT RUN

Start by tacking the underlay pads (1). The pile of the carpet should face down the stairs (gauge this by rubbing your palm along the carpet in both directions – it will feel smoother in the direction of the pile). Start at the bottom and lay it face down on the first tread. Tack it into place (2). Pull the carpet over the nosing and tack it to the base of the riser (3). Run the carpet upstairs, fixing it to grippers (4).

CARPETING WINDING STAIRS

Don't cut the carpet at all, but fold the excess under (1) and fix it to the risers with stair rods or long tacks.

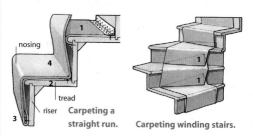

nosing

4

2

tread

riser

3

Carpeting a straight run.

Carpeting winding stairs.

ESTIMATING CARPET

To work out how much carpet you will need, measure the floor area and draw a freehand plan, including the position of doors, window bay, alcoves and so on, plus the full width of the doorframe. Make a note of the dimensions on the plan and take it to the flooring supplier, who will advise you on the most economical way to cover the floor.

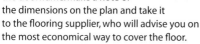

The ideal solution is to achieve a seamless wall-to-wall covering; but this is often impossible, either because a particular width is unobtainable or due to the fact that the room is such an irregular shape that there would be too much wastage if it were cut from one piece. Carpet has to be butted together in these circumstances – but try to avoid seams in the main walkways. You also have to consider matching the pattern and the direction of carpet pile: it must run in the same direction, or each piece of carpet will look different.

TIP: When measuring up before buying carpet remember to order 75 mm (3 in) extra all round for fitting.

Standard widths

Most manufacturers produce carpet to standard widths. Some can be cut to fit any shape of room, but the average wastage factor is reflected in the price of the carpet. Not all carpets are available in the

AVAILABLE WIDTHS

* 0.69 m (2 ft 3 in)
  0.91 m (3 ft)
  2.74 m (9 ft)
  3.66 m (12 ft)
* 4 m (13 ft)
* 4.57 m (15 ft)

* rare

full range of widths and you may have difficulty in matching a colour exactly from one width to another, so ask the supplier to check you can before buying.

Carpet is always made to metric sizes, but the imperial equivalent is the measurement that is normally quoted.

Carpet widths of 2.74 m (9 ft) and over are known as broadlooms; narrower widths are simply called body or strip carpets.

Carpet squares

Carpet squares – not to be confused with tiles – are large, rectangular loose-laid rugs. Simply order whichever size suits the proportions of your room. Carpet squares should be turned round from time to time to even out wear.

INDEX

If you have enjoyed this book, why not build on your expertise with other Collins titles?

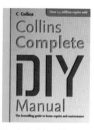

A revised edition of the most comprehensive DIY manual ever published.
552pp
£25
HB   0 00 718523 5

Key information for the DIY novice, all in the palm of your hand!
192pp
£4.99
PB   0 00 717603 1

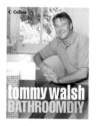

TV's favourite handyman takes an in-depth look at the bathroom.
128pp
£14.99
HB   0 00 715689 8

in the same series:
Kitchen DIY 0 00 715688 X
Outdoor DIY 0 00 715687 1
Living Spaces DIY 0 00 715686 3 (Oct 04)

To order any of these titles please telephone **0870 787 1732**
For further information about Collins books visit our website:
www.collins.co.uk